READING TERMINAL MARKET

An Illustrated History

DAVID K. O'NEIL

Camino Books, Inc.
Philadelphia

Manufactured in the United States of America

1 2 3 4 5 07 06 05 04

Library of Congress Cataloging-in-Publication Data

O'Neil, David K.
   Reading Terminal Market : an illustrated history / David K. O'Neil.
      p. cm.
Includes bibliographical references.
   ISBN 0-940159-78-3 (trade paper : alk. paper)
  1. Reading Terminal Market (Philadelphia, Pa.)--History. 2. Farmers' markets--Pennsylvania--Philadelphia--History. 3. Markets--Pennsylvania--Philadelphia--History. I. Title.
   HF5472.U7P56 2004
   381'.41'097481--dc22   2003016199

Unless otherwise noted, photographs are courtesy of the author.

Cover and interior design: Jerilyn Kauffman

The marks READING TERMINAL MARKET® and READING TERMINAL MARKET since 1893® are used with permission from the Reading Terminal Market Corporation.

Publisher
Camino Books, Inc.
P.O. Box 59026
Philadelphia, PA 19102

www.caminobooks.com

In memory of William Rembrandt Dimeling,
without whom there would be no Reading Terminal Market

CONTENTS

FOREWORD

The Market in the City—the City in the Market

What's wonderful about the Reading Terminal Market is that it has worked so well for so long. A combination of benign neglect and inspired improvisation has rendered it as vital and alive today as it was one hundred years ago.

We've been weekly users of the market for years and have amused ourselves off and on by trying to pinpoint the formal and functional qualities that make the market so appealing without ever becoming cute or clichéd. On the most basic level, one analogy we have found helpful is that of the American gridiron city. The gridiron pattern of streets and blocks is a pervasive model for most American cities, with its attributes of easy access, perceptual clarity, and its ability to accept tremendous variety in density, form, use, and architectural style. The market replicates in miniature the ground-level activity of Center City Philadelphia. Most of the uses are commercial, as they are on any typical American Main Street, and the individual stalls, with their different goods and signs, like the stores on Main Street, give the visual and commercial variety, which is at the heart of the success of the market as well as Main Street.

While Center City Philadelphia, over the last thirty years, has been redeveloped with little appreciation of the delights of variety and unexpected juxtapositions, the market has preserved these essential elements of the American City.

Robert Venturi, Steve Izenour, Daniel McCoubrey
Venturi, Scott-Brown and Associates

This piece was written in December 9, 1985, by the renowned Philadelphia firm that served as the project architect for much of Reading Terminal Market's restoration in the 1980s. The firm's principal, Robert Venturi, is the son of a produce wholesaler who frequently rented space in the market's cold-storage area.

ACKNOWLEDGMENTS

Thousands of merchants have set up stalls in Reading Terminal Market during the last 110 years and each one has a fascinating story. In spite of obstacle after obstacle they have endured with their humor intact, and the city is a better place because of them. They have completed over two billion transactions with hundreds of millions of customers, intimately linking the market to every community in the region.

The people at the "new" Reading Company were extraordinarily supportive of the market and all played a part either behind the scenes or "on the floor." It would be remiss not to thank: Earl McLeod, Doug Rogers, Jim Wunderle, Bob Boyle, Bill Becker, Tony Scoma, Chas Groshon, John Sebastian, Jerome Fulton, Michelle Insley, John Morris, Jacquie Firth, Jim Lavelle, Doug Humes, Jeff Algatt, Steve Park, Anne Nimick, Eugenia Warnock, Sally Powers, Grace Hall, Roseanne Giszynski, Cindy Mulaney, Bill Gardiner, Isaac Salter, Lenny Garvin, Bill Manion, Mary Kay Cavanaugh, Will Agate, Rick Cotten, Herman Cherry, Tony DeLeon, Felicity Taormina, Harry Yentzer, John Sullivan, Mike Skolyk, Ed Grimes, George Graham, Marion Brown, Aaron McLeod, Bill Hankowsky, Alfred Nebbio, Andrew Holloway, Chuck Carter, Ron Lankford, Joe Castle, John Seifert, Dick Kaplinsky, Patty Rucci, Christine O'Connor, John Lisle, Joanne Potts, Keith Jackson, Drew Lewis, and Rush Skakel.

Many of the photographs in the book were lent by market families whose lives are as much a part of the market's history as the trains and steel columns are. My thanks for their generosity go to Robert Moyer, William Ziegler, Noelle Margerum, Harry Ochs, Ernie Godshall, Michael Strange, Roger Bassett, Harvey Reilly, Blair Reilly, and George McKay's grandniece, Mary Holmes. Unless otherwise noted, photographs are courtesy of the author.

The curators and librarians at the Hagley Museum and Library, the Athenaeum of Philadelphia, and the Library Company of Philadelphia were as helpful as they were kind, and spending time at their institutions was a pleasure. Two contemporary market historians, Helen Tangires and Jay Barshinger, both wrote magnificent dissertations that added enormously to my understanding of the important role markets play in local economies.

Burk Uzzle, Anne Day, and Eli Albalancey see things that are extraordinary and have the talent to record them. Thank you all for lending such beautiful photographs. Christine Penrose, an artist, used her keen eye to help sort through thousands of market images and assisted me in choosing the ones for this book.

The good people at Project for Public Spaces in New York City deserve special thanks for encouraging me to write this book and for all they do to improve the public realm. And, of course, my parents, whose loyalty and interest in my market doings have encouraged me to forge on, in good times and bad, I thank most lovingly.

My brother and I were often taken to the market by our grandfather, Thomas P. O'Neil, who was city editor at the old *Philadelphia Record*. Without those early visits, I might never have wandered back in.

And, finally, this book was immeasurably improved by the editing skills of Michelle Scolnick and the assistance and suggestions of Barbara Gibbons from Camino Books.

READING TERMINAL MARKET CHRONOLOGY

1683	First recorded open-air market at Front and High Streets
1698–1835	Construction of market sheds on High Street
1833	State issues a charter to the Philadelphia and Reading Railroad Company
1859	All sheds removed from High Street
1860	Farmers' Market Company opens market hall
1864	Twelfth Street Market Company opens market hall
1889	
January	Reading discusses taking over Twelfth Street Market and Farmers' Market using the power of eminent domain
1891	
Jan. 15	City Council passes ordinance approving construction of Reading Terminal
April 3	Twelfth Street Market applies for injunction against Reading Company (injunction is denied)
May 1	$8 million in bonds approved for Reading Terminal project
May	Pennsylvania Supreme Court affirms Reading's eminent domain claim
Aug. 1	Reading Company settles with Farmers' Market for $600,000
Aug. 26	Reading Company settles with Twelfth Street Market for $400,000

1892

Feb. 11   Reading becomes largest rail system in the country

Feb. 20   Twelfth Street Market and Farmers' Market close

Feb. 22   Reading Terminal Market opens

1893

Jan. 29   First train enters Reading Terminal

July   Reading Terminal Market Cold Storage begins operating

1896   Foreclosure of Philadelphia and Reading Railroad Company

1897   Market ceiling completed

1902   First pay phone installed in Reading Terminal Market

1912   A&P opens first "economy store"

1923   George McKay, market's first superintendent, dies

1931   50 percent of market business conducted over the telephone

1934   Renovation of Twelfth Street windows and entrances

1938   Unions try to organize Reading Terminal Market

1942   Intersection of Eleventh and Market Streets is the busiest corner in the city, seeing 144,000 people a day

1947   Reading Terminal modernization

1952   Last steam train leaves the shed

1959   New food distribution center opens near airport

1959   Market 70 percent occupied and operating at a deficit

1959   Center City commuter rail connection first proposed

1960   Cold-storage area closes

1964   Reading Company threatens bankruptcy

1969   Market 55 percent occupied

1971   Reading Railroad declares bankruptcy

1976   Market 42 percent occupied

1976   Sam Rappaport subleases the market

1979   Market 20 percent occupied

1980   Reading Company emerges from bankruptcy and takes back control of the market

1983   Market 60 percent occupied

1984   Last train leaves the Reading Terminal, commuter tunnel opens

1985   Filbert Street façade and entrances restored

1986   Heat and air conditioning added in market

1989   Market 90 percent occupied

1990   Pennsylvania Convention Center buys Reading Terminal Market

1992   Market reconstructed by Convention Center

1992   Market celebrates 100th birthday

1993   Convention Center opens

1996   Nonprofit management company subleases market

2002   Market celebrates 110th birthday

A BRIEF HISTORY

The Early Markets in Philadelphia

To appreciate the history of Reading Terminal Market fully, one must go back to the earliest days of Philadelphia, when Twelfth and Filbert Streets were still woodland and there was a pond at Fourth and High Streets. Reading Terminal Market officially opened in February 1892, though it was over two hundred years in the making. This book traces the evolution of the market in its current location as part of a much longer story. Today's market at Twelfth and Filbert Streets is a direct descendant—architecturally, commercially, and socially—of a series of market halls, sheds, shambles, and open-air vendors that go back to the late 1600s.

Market Street was originally named High Street and remained so until 1859. High Street was planned by William Penn to be a commercial thoroughfare and was intentionally made wider than other city streets to handle trading activity. The name *High Street* derives from the Roman method of building roads with heavy stones raised above the surroundings to allow for drainage and for withstanding heavy use. Nearly every town or village in England has a High Street, which in most places is still the principal commercial street.

William Penn's England was full of markets, all integral to the local economy, streetscape, and way of life. Most English towns actually began as markets, a pattern repeated all over the world. In the New World, new markets reflected the cultures of the Old World, in architectural as well as vending styles.

The first markets on modern record in Philadelphia date from 1683, when an open-air market was established at Front and High Streets a year after William Penn founded the city. Philadelphia's first Clerk of the Market, Robert Brett, was appointed by the Municipal Councils in 1693. He collected fees and oversaw the opening and closing of the market, then at Second and High Streets, on Wednesdays and Saturdays beginning at seven o'clock in the morning after the ringing of the "butter bells" (bells rung to announce the opening). His responsibilities included ensuring that weights were fair and that hucksters (resellers, as opposed to farmers or producers) were kept at bay until two hours after the market had begun allowing the farmers first crack at selling.

At the time, the intersection of Second and High Streets was at the crest of a short hill, giving the market a natural vantage point over the broad landscape and river. In 1704 a small Watch House was built at the head of the market to keep an eye out for approaching vessels coming up the Delaware River and to make sure they were friendly. If any danger was seen, the market bell was rung to warn the townsfolk.

The market was not only the commercial center of the city, but the social and municipal center as well. Swelling with activity, it soon was unable to handle the crowds of a city growing in stature and population. In 1708 the city leaders decided to build a proper market house; the following year up went the headhouse, a two-and-a-half-story brick building, "the largest endeavor of our pilgrim fathers," with market sheds on the first floor and public spaces above.[1] A small east-facing balcony was used for speeches and announcements. The ground floor was open for foot traffic, and an auction room and stalls for millers and linen and stocking-makers from Germantown were placed in the four corners. A year later public stocks were added, reminding market traders of the consequences of short weights and customers of the dangers of picking pockets.

The proud edifice was not only the market hall; it was also the Great Town House or Guild Hall, the courthouse, and the meeting place of the legislature until the State House was built. The city was fanning out from the marketplace, the epicenter of what was soon to become the most powerful and influential city in the New World. The rules and regulations of the early market were forming the foundations of our modern municipal government.

Market activity continued to burgeon as more farmers and butchers carted wares to Second and High Streets. The market expanded not by plan but by need, and in 1722 the Common Council approved construction of more stalls up the center of High Street toward Third. As the markets grew so did the sophistication of city dwellers and in response to complaints, killing animals in the market was outlawed as part of the expansion program.

The following year Benjamin Franklin arrived in Philadelphia and must have gotten a good impression of the city's people and tastes as he strolled up High Street, wandering through the market stalls. In his later years, he even helped with some new designs to improve the look and sanitation of the markets. Franklin was undoubtedly won over by the markets, models of democracy and delicacy that they were, for when he became a property owner on High Street he remarked, "Considering our well-furnished plentiful market as the best of gardens, I am turning mine, in the midst of which my house stands, into grass plots and gravel walks with trees and flowering shrubs."[2]

Many of the goods that came to Philadelphia were from New Jersey, and a special market was constructed just for them. The Jersey Market was built in 1730 with a handsome headhouse and twenty stalls under a covered shed extending westward from Front Street toward Second. Situating the market near the river was also convenient for unloading fresh catch and for washing down the stalls at the end of the day. Because of heavy use—and abuse—the market was rebuilt in 1763 and again in 1822.

The early city was growing so fast that all the merchants who couldn't get stalls would set up illegally wherever they could, prompting complaints from adjacent property owners and concerned citizens. However, there was no denying that vendors served a demand, and the town fathers constantly intervened and built more markets and enacted more rules to control the commerce pushing into the hungry young city.

In 1745 the citizens in the "suburbs" at Second and Pine Streets deemed it inconvenient to travel to High Street to do their shopping and sought permission for the erection of their own market house. Two prosperous local landowners, Joseph Wharton and Edward Shippen, who foresaw that a good market could raise real estate values, fronted the proposal. The market was to be similar in style to the old Market Hall on Front Street, but more substantial. The market was quickly approved and built (that Mr. Shippen was mayor at the time probably helped to move matters along). New Market, as it came to be known, was extended another block south in 1809 to what was then Cedar Street (now South Street).

More people necessitated more markets. As the city's population grew, the High Street sheds were stretched to Third Street in 1759. In April 1764 a Fish Market was built in the middle of High Street, extending from the river to Front Street, where the Jersey Market began. Markets now stretched continuously from the river all the way to Third Street. The next year the Dock Street Market (midway between High Street and New Market) was authorized and the street was arched and graded to prepare for increased traffic and provide for proper runoff. The westward expansion of the sheds continued until 1821, when the markets reached all the way to Eighth Street. By 1830, sheds had even been built on High Street on the west side of Centre Square, from Fifteenth Street to Seventeenth Street.

The Rise of the Reading Railroad

During the same decade a new industry was gathering steam, and it would forever change the face of High Street, the markets, and the city. The railroad was coming to town, and High Street was eyed as a prime place to lay track. At first this was thought to be a bad idea because of the danger it posed to pedestrians and horses and the negative impact it would have on the market activity. There was discussion about putting the rails farther north or south. But ultimately a compromise was reached, and the rails were laid alongside the market sheds on High Street. Many of the sheds' eaves had to be shortened to allow for safe passage of the trains. Train engines were not permitted to run on their own steam in the city, so railcars were pulled by horses or mules up High Street to Broad Street, then north to Callowhill Street and west to the Schuylkill River, where they connected with the main lines that ran up to coal country.

In 1833 the state issued a charter to the Philadelphia and Reading Railroad Company (often referred to simply as Reading) to build a rail connection between its two namesake cities. It was essentially a "coal road" that began operations between Pottstown and Philadelphia, a distance of forty-three miles, in 1838. The railroad company opened its first terminal in 1839 at the southeast corner of Broad and Cherry Streets. Designed to look important, it was three stories tall with a cupola, a clock tower, and an adjoining car shed.

The railroad would move its terminal four times. In 1850 a terminal was constructed on Broad Street above Vine. In 1860 the railroad erected a larger depot at Broad and Callowhill Streets that covered an entire city block, and then in the late 1870s it moved to Ninth and Green Streets into what was originally the depot for the Philadelphia, Germantown and Norristown Railroad. This location was also chosen for its strategic connections with other lines, recently acquired by Reading to win a larger share of the growing demand for coal—the "black diamond"—which Reading was determined to move more of than anyone else. The railroad's last Philadelphia terminal would rise at Twelfth and Market Streets.

Railroads were a boon for farmers and vendors. The rails brought in new trade and made it easier for market vendors from the outlying counties to get to market. A round-trip that once took three days by horse now could be made in one long day. But the markets and their old-fashioned ways were seen as anachronistic, not fitting for a progressive city. They were considered dangerous, unsanitary harbors for unseemly characters, and a movement was afoot to have them permanently removed. Such talk had gone on almost from the very beginning, but now the voices of dissent were growing louder.

Historic scrapbooks chronicling the issues of the time first describe the market sheds as a nuisance in 1852. The newly consolidated city opened a Market Department in 1854, further fanning debate among detractors about the fate of the sheds. The "new" city was modernizing and the old markets were a reminder of the past, in the way of the future. Attitudes were changing.

From the Sheds to the Halls

A new form of market was setting the standard for the city's changing tastes: elegant buildings with high ceilings for good ventilation, paved floors with spacious aisles, and vendors behind the counters who actually owned the markets as stockholders. Many markets were quite ornate, with none of the shabbiness of the old sheds. These new-style indoor markets came into vogue in the 1850s, and as the best of the farmers, butchers, and vendors left the sheds in High Street and set up in the "halls" the decline of the old street sheds accelerated. Emptiness added to the squalor, and the call for their removal seemed all but inevitable. There were diehards, though, and a Market Protection League was formed to lobby for the continuation of the sheds.

Newspaper reports of the time indicated a rising sentiment against the preservation of the narrow sheds running up High Street. It seemed the markets had outlived their usefulness and were publicly derided as places where "everything has gone wrong since hair powder fell out of fashion."[3] The opponents of the sheds now included many of the old marketers themselves, citizens who detested their filth, firefighters who argued they couldn't maneuver around them, and the streetcar industry, which wanted the rights of way to drive through them. That industry was getting more powerful by the day, and what with its influence and the desire of the populace for this new form of transportation, the end of the sheds was imminent.

In April 1859 the city decided to put an end to the "ancient encumbrances" on High Street. The sheds were to be put out of use at the end of October, giving the farmers one last season to sell and time to look for another place. The sheds were taken down in November and December of that year. After the sheds were removed, the name of High Street was changed commemoratively to Market Street.

There was not much fretting over the loss of the sheds, and a scrapbook of the day gushed with a description of the newly opened Western Market House at Sixteenth and Market Streets as one that "outrivals Quincy Market" in Boston, with seven north–south aisles, 280 stalls with countertops made of the finest Italian marble, and "perfect ventilation."[4]

By 1854 two large, indoor markets had already opened on the east side of Broad Street below Race, and on Race Street at the southwest corner of Juniper Street. By 1860 more new market halls had been built and it was said that Philadelphia had "four miles of markets," including both indoor and outdoor venues. The city still owned and operated street markets on Bainbridge, Spring Garden, Callowhill, Girard, Wharton, and North Second Streets, as well as the one that remains today, the market at Second and Pine Streets that some people still refer to as New Market.

The new generation of market halls included the antecedents of Reading Terminal Market, the Farmers' Market and the Twelfth Street Market. Originally, two groups of organizers, farmers and butchers, had reached a tacit agreement to purchase property on Tenth Street just south of Market Street for a market hall. For reasons not entirely clear, the butchers decided to go it alone and broke off from the farmers. Having been "frozen out" by their supposed allies, the farmers—in true competitive fashion, and, with the impending closure of the sheds, needing to acquire a place to do business—decided to open their own market and bought prime mid-block property on the north side of Market Street between Eleventh and Twelfth Streets.

An imposing structure was planned and financed by the stallholders, who incorporated and called themselves the Farmers' Market Company. They moved quickly and opened on Market Street in 1860. Their hall extended all the way to Filbert Street, making it the largest market in the city. Market shareholders were farmers, poulterers, fishmongers, other butchers, and vendors from Philadelphia and the surrounding counties who were looking for an alternative to setting up in the sheds or peddling their wares all over the city from the backs of horse-drawn market wagons. The market was modern in every way and even had forty apartments "fitted with beds and toilet apparatus which were regularly occupied by farmers who bring their produce to the stalls the night before market day" on the northern end of the market.[5] A railroad spur running down the west side of the building added to its convenience.

Things did not go as well for the butchers at the Franklin Market on Tenth Street. Even though the market was completely occupied, sales were poor. A beautifully carved statue of Benjamin Franklin that stood watch over the entranceway was unable to provide divine guidance to get the market into high gear. (Today this statue is in the entrance to the Public Ledger Building at Sixth and Chestnut Streets.) These butchers saw the success of the farmers' market just around the corner and started to make plans to move onto the same block and go head to head with their nemeses.

The butchers named their new enterprise the Twelfth Street Market Company (often referred to as the Franklin Market Company) and incorporated in April 1864 with assets of $114,691. The market house on Tenth Street was sold to the Mercantile Library. The incorporators worked in conjunction with a market developer, John Rice. Rice was something of a market entrepreneur of the day; in 1853 he had developed the Race Street Market, one of the first new-style market halls built in the city.

Rice and the Twelfth Street Market Company agreed on terms, with Rice holding a controlling interest in the market. Stalls were fitted out and the market opened on October 1, 1864.

Moving from the intimate, narrow, low-ceilinged sheds, rife with the spice of ages, into the soaring, majestic new market halls represented a major evolutionary move for the old market culture. The new markets were sophisticated, tasteful, and grand. Light poured in through large windows (the invention of plate glass was a big advancement that revolutionized commercial architecture and the retail experience) and marketgoers, tired of having to shout over the din of streetcars, step over stray cats, dodge pigeons, push away unruly wags, and sidle alongside smelly drunks to get their vittles, followed en masse. It was a whole new shopping experience, and customers spoke with their pocketbooks as they patronized the new, indoor, lit, ventilated, decorated, and downright showplace-like market houses.

By 1876, Philadelphia was awash in national attention with the Centennial. It was an industrial and agricultural leader and its markets were said to be the best in the country. A guidebook of the day listed twenty-eight privately owned market houses and seven street markets owned by the city. The markets were listed prominently in all the guidebooks for "strangers and citizens" alike.

Today, it is hard to imagine that Philadelphia was once an agricultural powerhouse and in 1850 the top market-garden–producing county in the entire United States, slipping to number three in 1860. By 1879 it had dropped to sixth place (Queens, New York, was number one) but still had 780 farms listed on the census with 35,902 acres under production out of a total 87,000 acres in the entire city. William Penn's "greene Country Towne" was still visibly quite green indeed.

Philadelphia was producing mass quantities of its own food, and market habitués valued local farmers and their fresh goods above all. Market selections were not limited to what was in season, however, with frequent visits by schooners from the West Indies, Central and South America, the Mediterranean, and Asia bearing sugar, coffee, pineapples, oranges and lemons. "Fusion cuisine" was popular even then, and Chester County lamb was as apt to be cooked with spices from the Orient as with mint from Roxborough.

The market system in the city provided a sturdy network for commerce, community, and cultural exchange. Like little village markets anywhere in the world, Philadelphia's marketplaces were the center points of neighborhoods. The nineteenth-century markets were still largely farmers' (or producers') markets, although hucksters were common as well. The farmers had always been welcomed, valued even, by city dwellers who counted on the steady supply of local products.

The Reading Goes to Market Street

The Reading Railroad, meanwhile, had been busily building a rather formidable network of its own. In the early 1880s its chief rival, the Pennsylvania Railroad, had built an enormous, modern train shed and headquarters on the southwest corner of Broad and Filbert Streets. By contrast, the Reading's terminal at Ninth Street was remote. The passenger trade was becomingly increasing profitable, and Reading was not going to sit back and watch the Pennsylvania Railroad punch tickets. The brash, established, and audacious Reading Railroad knew it had to be closer to the action in the center of the city.

By 1888 Reading had identified Twelfth and Market Streets as the site it wanted for the new terminal of the "Reading road" and had incorporated a separate company, the Philadelphia and Reading Railway Company, to act at its behest. The Twelfth and Market site was publicly debated and some people thought the terminal should be allowed to go only to Arch Street, with a large plaza in front joining it visually and aesthetically to Market Street. Reading argued that the terminal would remove dangerous grade crossings and provide great public good, and therefore deserved powers of eminent domain, which were meant for such civic undertakings.

The project was big news. People quickly took sides, and issues and deals and dollars flew all over the place. The Farmers' and Twelfth Street Markets were threatened, but the stallholders probably were not surprised. Reading's idea had been floating about for quite some time, and market vendors had to have known about it for a while and had time to assess their strategic position. They owned the real estate along with some outside shareholders such as John Rice and, it was speculated, Reading itself, which had quietly been buying up shares in both markets.

In November 1889 Reading ordered stock reports of the Twelfth Street Market Company and the Farmers' Market Company from Harrisburg. Two months later, on January 16, 1890, the ordinance for the new Reading road and terminal at Twelfth and Market was finally introduced in City Council. Public sentiment was shifting toward the Reading plan and the politicians knew it. Reading worked diligently throughout the year lobbying support, buying real estate, and advancing engineering and design work.

The president of the Reading sent a letter to City Council in December 1890 pleading his case once again: "The Reading Company suffers greatly, in common with the public, from the location of its inconvenient and unsuitable passenger stations . . . all of which are too far distant from the centers of trade and travel. . . ." There was in fact growing public sentiment for the raised-road concept that would eliminate grade crossings from busy city streets. So finally, after years of deliberations, Reading's ordinance was formally approved by City Council on December 26, 1890.

The markets smelled big trouble. In the first week of January 1891, Archibald Angus McLeod, onetime trainman and newly installed president of the Reading Railway, received a letter from an attorney representing the shareholders of the Twelfth Street Market Company requesting a meeting. The meeting did not go well and in March 1891, the board of directors of the Twelfth Street Market authorized the filing of an injunction, if needed. Reading responded immediately by proceeding with condemnation of the Twelfth Street Market Company property. The market countered with an application for an injunction, which was summarily denied.

In May, both the Farmers' and Twelfth Street Markets asked for a meeting with McLeod. There were motivations on both sides of the table to come to an agreement. The planned "raised" railroad track and terminal, twenty feet above ground level, allowed for the possibility of relocating the market at street level below the train shed. The clock was ticking for Reading, which wanted to remove the markets as quickly as possible and actually invited the stallholders to be part of the new terminal complex. This was an attractive offer especially considering the cold-storage operation that was being planned for the terminal's basement. The market vendors wanted to avoid a lengthy and costly legal battle and disruption to their livelihood, and they knew they had a better bargaining position with the railroad than they would if they were evicted through eminent domain. Reading knew from the stock papers what both companies were worth, and McLeod offered to buy them out.

Negotiations continued over the summer. McLeod negotiated individually with both markets and made headway with the Farmers' Market, whose shareholders agreed to sell out entirely for $600,000 at the beginning of August. The idea of a new market with cooled basement storage must have been appealing to many of the tenants, especially in the middle of the summer.

The deal with the Farmers' Market and the growing momentum of the Reading Terminal project gave McLeod the upper hand. The more divided Twelfth Street Market was holding out and McLeod sent the shareholders a letter two days after settling with the Farmers' Market, offering $400,000 cash and the "present tenants of your market the preference so as they may desire to avail themselves of the same, in renting the stalls and other appliances in the new market."[6]

Reading Terminal Market Takes Shape

The shareholders met again and tentatively agreed to McLeod's offer—if Reading guaranteed their market would remain open and not be shut down for demolition or construction. McLeod agreed to the stipulation, and a vote was scheduled among the shareholders of the Twelfth Street Market on August 26, 1891. There were 1,233 votes cast in favor of the Reading offer, and only 425 shareholders were opposed. By the following week, the first of the terminal's great arches was in place on the northern end of the shed as the market took shape below.

Even during the last phases of negotiations with the markets, Reading was not in a holding pattern. On the block between Filbert and Arch Streets, demolition and site preparation had taken place, the train shed's foundation had been laid, and the exterior granite walls were already up. The shells of the market and basement were essentially complete. The market vendors didn't have to read the newspaper; the train was at their door, and it seemed unstoppable. The noise and smoke from the construction equipment, visible out their back doors, must have added to their frustration and sense of futility in trying to stop the "Reading road."

The next five months were extraordinarily busy. Final agreements were drawn up, shareholders bought out, the new market and cold-storage area planned, stalls assigned, and leases put into final form, and Reading essentially took over the operation of the markets. In a November 3, 1891, memo to President McLeod, J. H. Loomis, the director of real estate for the Reading wrote, "I have taken charge of the Farmers Market Company."

The new market (referred to as the Filbert Street Market before it opened) was well under way, and Reading decided an experienced hand was needed to oversee its completion. The company contacted George H. McKay, superintendent of the Center Market in the District of Columbia, and offered him the job. McKay was born in Maine to an American mother and a Canadian father who was a fisherman from Nova Scotia, a fact that was probably not lost on President McLeod, a Canadian by birth.

The Center Market, originally incorporated by the U.S. Congress and completed in 1877, was owned and operated by the Washington Market Company. It claimed to be "the largest, best ventilated and most imposing market structure in this country if not the world."[7] Located at Seventh and Pennsylvania Avenues, the market was torn down in the 1920s. The National Archives Building now occupies the site.

The challenge of building the newest and largest indoor market in the country enticed McKay. The Center Market was 57,000 square feet and the Reading Market was going to be almost 50 percent larger with a basement of equal size for cold storage. McKay accepted Reading's offer of $2,400 per year and a pension, almost double what he was making in Washington, and departed for Philadelphia on December 31, 1891. His brother Edwin would soon follow to oversee the cold-storage part of the operation.

George McKay began work on January 1, 1892. The market was nearing completion and would open in less than two months. President McLeod must have been pleased to have the superintendent's job filled, as he was busy running a railroad and angling to control the lucrative coal market. The last thing he needed was a bunch of meetings about meat hooks and counter heights.

Even as construction roared ahead, there were still nagging legal problems. A suit was filed by a splinter group of Twelfth Street Market shareholders who challenged the "pooled stock" of their fellow stockholders who had agreed to sell to Reading. The challenge held up the dissolution of the Twelfth Street Market Company, but not the sale to Reading.

The lawsuit was but a minor distraction for the railroad during the construction of the terminal. It was a massive project that involved the leading financiers, architects, and engineers in the country. Francis H. Kimball, an architect from New York, was consulted on the ornamentation of the building's exterior, and Wilson Brothers and Company of Philadelphia were the lead engineers and prepared all of the drawings. Journalists were allowed to see the plans and the *Philadelphia Record* newspaper predicted the terminal would be "the handsomest structure of its kind in America. . . . The building will more resemble a magnificent opera house or public library than a railway station . . . making the structure one of the greatest adornments of Philadelphia."[8]

The building was unquestionably solid, engineered to bear the load of thirteen steam engines and rows of cars on thirteen tracks directly above the market. The span of the shed was to be the largest in the world at 266 feet, with a height that would reach 88 feet. Some of the materials used to create the monumental rail headquarters are worth noting briefly, for their sheer grandiosity:

50 million pounds of iron
10 million board feet of oak, hemlock, and white and yellow pine
16 million Philadelphia-made bricks
135,000 square feet of glass
180,000 square feet of tin roofing
50,000 square feet of Vermont and Italian marble
15,000 square feet of majolica
22 elevators
125 miles of pipe to service the cold-storage area alone

If Archibald Angus McLeod wanted to show the world that the Reading Company was making a break with its past, the terminal would surely mark a new era. And his rail and coal empire was just about to get a whole lot bigger.

On February 11, 1892, news of the terminal's construction was eclipsed by above-the-fold headlines in newspapers across the country. McLeod had just pulled off the greatest railroad deal ever consummated in the United States. The previous day he had made deals to acquire the Lehigh Valley Railroad and the Jersey Central Railroad, making Reading's system the largest in the country and giving Reading control of the anthracite (hard coal) business. That was like cornering the oil market today. Reading was now a powerhouse, and the majesty of the terminal seemed more and more fitting for the company.

The merchant kings of cabbage and kale were getting ready for their new "house" as well. The market vendors were preparing for their final week of business in the old halls on Market Street. They would continue serving customers without the loss of even a day, as McLeod had promised. The rear portion of the Farmers' Market that housed the apartments was already being demolished, however, and Reading had a double shift on the project working around the clock. Just one block north, between Filbert and Arch Streets, the scene was all charcoal smoke, thumping machinery, and noisy shouts as workers put the final pieces for the new market into place. Customers were drawn that last week to witness the passing of the thirty-year-old markets and to marvel at the gargantuan shed and, of course, the new market house.

The last market day, Saturday, February 20, was surprisingly normal. Nearly all the stalls were laden with the best of everything, and butchers' hooks groaned with carcasses of mutton and beef. Buyers flocked in for a last purchase and the day was reported to be one of the busiest ever, notwithstanding a tinge of sadness and nostalgia.

At the close of business, there was an immediate transition to get ready for moving day and Charles McCaul, the contractor hired by Reading to build the station, was on hand with his crews to assist. A temporary track was laid over Filbert Street, and vendors who had leased stalls in the new market loaded their fixtures and goods onto freight carts and rolled them across the street. The new stalls were not yet built, so the old stalls were moved into the new market and set up for the interim. The work went on all night, and there was a good crowd of onlookers who watched with the help of a temporary lighting system that added to the drama.

On Monday, February 22, 1892, the new market opened without much fanfare. Vendors could look out the market doors and watch the last walls of their old markets tumble into piles of rubble. The new market was still a bit makeshift. It had a temporary roof that was not exactly leakproof, but because the train shed was still being constructed, the merchants would have to make do with the roof for at least another year. The floor was made of asphalt, not concrete, for the winter weather was too cold for pouring concrete. The cold-storage area was not yet operable. The grandeur of the new market was not fully evident.

Nonetheless, the market rapidly filled with vendors and within a month it was almost 70 percent occupied. Contracts were awarded in March for 680 stalls (out of a total of 800) to be made of oak, iron, tile, and marble. Eight thousand iron meat hooks were ordered for the 400 stalls allotted to meat and poultry. The new layout had twelve aisles that ran from east to west, four aisles that ran from north to south, and stalls around the perimeter, with those at the eastern end specially designed and reserved for fishmongers. The ceiling was eighteen feet high and there were eight elevators that serviced the basement cold-storage area, the market, and the train floor.

Vendors from other markets around the city came to make their own inspections, and many of them signed leases. By September all of the fish stalls were rented, and in November a group of seventeen vendors from the Eastern Market on Fifth Street (now the site of the Bourse Building) signed up for forty-six stalls.

By the time the first train rolled into the Reading Terminal on January 29, 1893, the market was nearly full. New stalls, a new roof, and cold storage that could keep meat chilled to just the right temperature year round provided the ideal combination to attract hordes of customers. Not only had the railroad entered a new era; so had urban food-buying and -selling. In its first year the terminal handled about 294 trains each day, and many of the millions of passengers came to know and love the market.

The Cold-Storage Revolution

The basement cold-storage system was ready by July 1893 and was considered a true marvel. The entire area, except for a wide passageway on the perimeter, was filled with cold rooms ranging in size from 5,000 to 17,000 cubic feet. The ceiling height in the rooms was just less than seven feet, and each room could be individually controlled with a range of temperatures from three to forty-four degrees Fahrenheit. It was particularly important that air be kept dry, and this was achieved through the use of a series of air locks on the doors, which closed automatically. The lumber used was dressed spruce, chosen because it didn't impart any smells to articles in storage. A ceiling-mounted roller system of iron tracks allowed goods to be moved easily on hangers through the corridors and into the cold rooms. The "weather," as it was called, was actually ammoniated brine, which was produced mechanically and circulated by centrifugal pumps through miles and miles of coils.

The system was so effective that it was said an egg stored in one of the cold rooms for up to fourteen months would still be perfect and could be sold as fresh. It wasn't cheap to run, though, and actually cost more to operate than the market upstairs. The basement required a larger staff than the market itself, and early payrolls show a team of engineers, inspectors, clerks, elevator attendants, and a superintendent, George McKay's younger brother Edwin, also known as Nash. Vendors didn't mind paying extra rent for the use of the cold storage, because it allowed them to sell a huge selection of products year round and helped to solidify the market's reputation as the place to find everything for the well-stocked larder.

The Reading Railroad advertised a number of cold-storage facilities throughout its system, but the market basement was its showplace and it proudly offered tours on Wednesdays and Thursdays. They were quite popular, especially on hot summer days.

The basement was used by many market tenants as well as by outsiders such as restaurants, caterers, and food manufacturers. Hospitals stored serums and medicines there. Local breweries (including Yuengling) stored hops. Well-to-do families with big appetites and big pocketbooks, such as the Wideners, rented space for personal use. Bulb companies liked the precision of the temperature controls and stored tens of thousands of lilies in the cool, dark rooms, ready to be brought out and forced in time for Easter.

Mechanical cold storage changed the way food was handled and the way it was financed. A farmer or a dealer with a cold-storage lease could "take it to the bank" and get a business loan. The perishable nature of the retail fresh-food business had previously made such loans risky and unavailable. This was one of the major innovations that would also spawn the growth of supermarkets and the consolidation of small food producers to create larger and larger "corporations." Mechanical cold-storage systems were expensive to build, but they were destined to succeed and would revolutionize how food got from the farmer to the consumer. Reading Terminal Market was not first in using the mechanical system—many other cold-storage facilities already existed, including one beneath the Brooklyn Bridge—but the combination of cold storage with a retail market and train station was a first.

Another major factor that helped to supply markets in Philadelphia and the rest of the northeast in the 1890s was the growth of truck farming in the South. Market gardeners in Florida, Georgia, Alabama, and South Carolina found ready markets for early vegetables up north and sent loads of product via steamers and rail to Philadelphians longing for a taste of spring.

A useful adjunct to the market's cold storage in the basement was a subsystem that pumped chilled brine through coils up to counters on the market floor. Tenants who wanted a little "minifridge" at their stall or who wanted chilled display counters just had to pay a monthly refrigeration fee and ask Nash McKay to "tap in." The counters were also designed for ice blocks to keep products cool. There are still a few of these old "refrigerated" units on the market floor today. One is at Frankenfield's Poultry, formerly Godshall's on Fourth Avenue.

Ice was another commodity made and sold by the cold-storage plant. In 1894, after the kinks had been worked out of the cold storage system, Reading installed a twenty-ton piece of machinery that was capable of making twenty-eight tons of ice a day. The vendors enthusiastically endorsed the move and no longer had to haul in their own ice or get deliveries from outside firms. The ice operation was large enough to service the needs of the market, the railroad, and neighborhood stores and restaurants.

Demand boomed for the cold-storage area and new rooms were continually added in the basement. The central location of the facility, the direct elevator access to the trains, and the efficiency of the operation made it even more desirable. One of the earliest clients of the cold storage was Bassett's Ice Cream, one of the upstairs market's original tenants. Bassett's rented its own room, just next to the elevator near the northeast corner, in 1898, and began manufacturing ice cream on site; it would continue doing so for another sixty-three years.

Vendors from the old Twelfth Street and Farmers' Markets who decided to make the move must have been thrilled with the new market's innovations. Reading Terminal Market was then the largest market in the city, and what with the steady streams of commuter passengers, innovative cold storage, and a brand-new facility, there was little to complain about.

Growing Pains

But there were some problems. Number one was the roof. When the market was first occupied, it had a temporary roof during construction of the train shed and didn't receive a "permanent" roof until 1897. The market roof was really a ceiling; the actual roof was the giant barrel-shaped shed covering the thirteen tracks. The market ceiling was constructed to catch and route the water from the open-ended shed and train tracks immediately overhead. The original passenger walkways between the trains in the shed were partly made of glass block to allow natural light into the market (there were also skylights in the shed roof). Unfortunately, more than light was finding its way into the market: there were almost immediate reports of leaks onto the stalls and stallholders. At the time, one butcher was said to hold an umbrella as he conducted business. Things got so bad that the entire ceiling had to be rebuilt in 1901. It was done section by section to minimize disruption. The glass block on the walkways upstairs was also removed in hopes of alleviating the leaks, but the problem was going to be persistent, as many of the old-time tenants will confirm.

Another large problem was the sudden bankruptcy of the Reading Railroad in 1893. Archibald Angus McLeod's empire came down hard, and he resigned in September 1893 after a brief but dramatic tenure at the helm. The Reading Terminal was built largely as a result of his vision and persistence; his correspondence reveals that he was involved in the smallest details of the market even while he was working on some of the largest business deals in the world. Reading was such a large company that the effects of its bankruptcy are said to have been a major factor in precipitating a nationwide depression. Even though the company was placed in receivership, the operations of the market remained relatively unscathed. In fact, the operating records of the time indicate a decade of healthy growth during the dark period of depression for much of the country. People do have to eat, and markets can actually do well in a down economy. By 1896 a new holding company had been formed, and the Reading Terminal was leased to the newly named Philadelphia and Reading Railway Company (it had been called the Philadelphia and Reading *Railroad* Company). None other than the reigning titan of the time, J. Pierpont Morgan, largely masterminded the reorganization of the company, and one can only wonder if he was seduced by the delicacies of the market on his trips to Philadelphia.

Another great figure of the day who enjoyed traipsing through Reading Terminal Market was John Wanamaker, who coincidentally was a major investor in the Reading Railroad. His store later had the contract to produce the Stotesbury china (so named because it was designed by the wife of one of the Reading's presidents, Edward T. Stotesbury) used in the railroad's dining cars.

The market's early years were marked by full occupancy and a reputation for quality. More and more wholesale business was being conducted with restaurants, hotels, and institutions. Orders were shipped out by rail and truck all over the country. By 1900, the Reading Company was running a parcel-post business in the terminal called the U.S. Express Parcel Company, and 75 percent of its business was from Reading Terminal Market, which was shipping over a thousand baskets a week. The parcel company was expanded and moved closer to Filbert Street to be more convenient for servicing orders from the merchants. The Pennsylvania Railroad even sent delivery boys over to the market to pick up orders for clients on its Main Line branch.

Weather was very much an issue in the market because it had no heating system and air conditioning hadn't been invented yet. Many merchants built offices above their stalls and used small oil stoves to provide a modicum of heat for clerks. There were complaints about the fumes and the possibility of fire, so in 1902 gas was brought into the market for the first time and piped to twenty mezzanine-level offices.

Telephones were made available the same year when Reading installed a junction box in the market. No longer would orders have to be sent over by messenger or through the mail; the telephone allowed merchants to speak directly and instantly with customers. The market had the finest and best selection of goods in the region, and customers were confident that anything from the farmers and purveyors was going to be of the highest quality.

The vendors were as important as the market building or the products. The personal relationships established in the market helped build an extremely loyal clientele and a deeply satisfying aspect to the job. The market was virtually full after the first year, with butchers leasing the greatest number of stalls. The market would continue to be fully leased for the next sixty years, although there would be a gradual and general trend to larger leaseholds for all categories of tenants and a reduction in the total number of standholders. In the first decade there were an incredible 380 vendors in all, specializing as follows: 150 produce farmers, 35 produce dealers, 4 produce wholesalers, 25 poulterers, 6 fishmongers, 100 butchers, 25 butter and egg stalls, 1 flower stand, 3 flour and meal vendors, 29 specialty grocers and provisioners, 1 stationery store, and 1 coffee, tea, and spice business. The early-morning hubbub must have been intense, especially during the growing season, when the market swelled with local farmers.

More rooms for cold storage were built in 1905, bringing the total volume under refrigeration to 284,000 cubic feet. The ceiling was six feet nine inches high, meaning that the basement housed just over 42,000 square feet of refrigerated rooms. The basement was a warren of rooms, aisles, and doors straight out of a painting by Hieronymous Bosch, with a low, brick, barrel-vaulted ceiling, coated in many areas with a thick, dark chocolate–colored cork. Goods were brought down by elevator from Track One and Track Thirteen (the easternmost and westernmost tracks) and by hand down stairs and chutes on Filbert Street and Arch Street and along the back driveway just west of Eleventh Street. The loading and service entrances were on the east side, where goods would be weighed in or assigned a cold-storage room. There was a platform scale big enough to hold one of the steel wheeled baggage carts from the train shed. In the early days of the cold-storage area, ice once formed so fast on the ceiling of one of the rooms that it started to rise and pushed up the market floor itself, causing serious damage.

New Challenges

The fortunes of the market remained steady for many years and didn't begin to tip until the Great Depression. But even then, the market was full, cold-storage demand was increasing, and some of the merchants had grown to be among the largest wholesalers in the city. The tip was seen more outside the market. Philadelphia's days as the "workshop of the world" were over. The closing of factories, job losses, the growing popularity of the automobile, and increasing suburbanization all brought new challenges to the market.

The consolidating food industry was experimenting with a new retail form, the supermarket, and one even opened directly across Twelfth Street from Reading Terminal Market. The Great Atlantic and Pacific Tea Company, which was to become a giant in the supermarket industry, started as bulk tea merchandisers in 1859. When the founder's son took over the business he went for the cash-and-carry trade and began opening "economy stores" in 1912. Within two years he had opened another sixteen hundred and by 1930 the company had over fifteen thousand stores.

Another big problem that was going to continue to plague the market for the foreseeable future was parking. The merchants banded together in 1930 and formed the Reading Terminal Market Merchants Association, realizing that something had to be done about the "city's drastic parking regulations, which were driving customers away by the thousands."[9] The merchants implemented a free-parking program, began a cooperative advertising campaign, and started to work on promotions to attract new patrons.

The Reading Terminal Market Merchants Association planned an annual series of "Food Show and Home Progress Exhibitions" beginning in 1931. The first one was ceremonially opened by Mayor Harry A. Mackey and programs included "a hundred decorated booths, cooking demonstrations, marketing talks, musical novelties and daily addresses on the various phases of a public market."[10] Clearly, the market intended to solidify its favorable position with the public and to differentiate itself from the new competition.

The market was still doing a substantial business over the phone and by mail. Orders were called in and sent out hourly on "ultra-modern" refrigerated trucks, which serviced the three million people within a thirty-mile radius of the market. The new market superintendent, George H. Ettien (who took over after the death of George McKay in 1923), said, "We ship food to faraway mountain resorts. Our daily orders go to at least 38 states as well as Canada, Mexico and France. Fifty percent of our business is done over the telephone and I think this newfangled system is wrong for many reasons."[11] He lamented the fact that new housewives didn't frequent the market and advocated educating them about the benefits of visiting the market in person and learning firsthand about value and quality.

The Reading Company bolstered the merchants' strategy and funded the market's first major renovation since its opening. New entrances and windows were installed on Twelfth Street in 1934, storage rooms were added in the basement, and the ice-making machinery was modernized. New awnings and graphics were developed to give the market a contemporary look. A fish aquarium was also built inside the market as an attraction. The new windows were refrigerated and were made attractive with special electric lights and displays of delicacies from all parts of the world: deer meat from the Arctic, rare nuts from the tropics, luscious fruits from Brazil, and other exotic foods from China, India, and Arabia.

Cornelius Weygandt, a professor of English at the University of Pennsylvania, wrote in his 1938 book of essays *Philadelphia Folks* that the market was "one of the seven wonders of Philadelphia" and "all the world is tributary to the [Reading Terminal] Market." A thorough reading of his essay reveals a certain sense of loss, though, as he adds that "it is idle to pretend that food even in this [Reading Terminal] Market, as good a market as there is in this country, is as good as it averaged yesterday." He quotes from vendors who confide that "sales are not as good as they used to be."

Fewer farmers and more hucksters or middlemen were behind the counters. There was more variety, but less direct selling. Cold storage could keep things available year round, but it could also dry out meats and draw flavor from vegetables best eaten the day they are picked. The market was inexorably being sucked into the new food-buying arena that was to be dominated by the supermarkets. A certain quaintness became the calling card of the market, and it was no longer the marvel of decades past. The market was still dominant—butchers and farmers still made the long trip to the city with primroses from Frankford and scrapple from Chester County, the stalls were full, and it made a profit for the railroad—but it was being challenged by forces of change that it had little control over.

Union organizers swooped into the market in the late 1930s and signed up a smattering of employees. As further efforts to unionize the market were stymied, a strike was called and a picket line went up around the block. Truck drivers bringing products to the market refused to cross the line even though the strike didn't begin until nine o'clock in the morning, and most deliveries had already been made for the day. The unions claimed the market was a closed shop, and merchants counter-charged with claims of intimidation.

Periodic skirmishes with unions continued through the war years. Rival unions, the American Federation of Labor (AFL) and the Congress of Industrial Organizations (CIO), vied for loyalty, and each tried to organize the entire market. Additional walkouts and strikes were called, which did not help the flow of business. Many of the market's butchers were union members, but most vendors were not. Some of the merchants felt that their businesses had been permanently damaged. The market was really being used as a public political arena by the unions that were fighting a much larger turf battle throughout the city.

The war years brought food shortages. Rationing of meat, fats, oils, cheese, and butter was put into effect. Big meat-packing houses in the Midwest went on strike and the shortages became even more acute. The market was one of the few places in the city with a supply line of local pork, beef, veal, and butter, and thousands flocked to Twelfth and Filbert Streets hoping to make a purchase. On May 9, 1946, a newspaper reported that twelve thousand eager buyers arrived at the market in the early morning and waited outside, looking longingly through the windows that were no longer full of abundant displays. It was the largest crowd in the history of the market, and nearly one hundred police officers and mounted patrols were called in to keep the peace. The lines continued for months and were generally peaceful, although there were a few overzealous customers, including one woman, according to reports, who hit a man over the head with a leg of lamb as he tried to cut in..

Pierce and Schurr Meats established its partnership in 1943 and made a small fortune during the shortages because Earl Schurr, a longtime market tenant, had a local supply line of meat from farmers in Montgomery County. Morris Pierce, who had gotten his start in the market many years earlier with William Margerum, was hired and made a partner by Schurr when Schurr expanded his business. Their market counters were among the few places in the city with any volume of products, and they sold out shortly after they opened each day.

Meanwhile, the Reading Railroad had experienced uninterrupted profits since climbing out of bankruptcy at the turn of the century. In the mid-1940s it had over twenty thousand employees and was still a major force. The railroad business had changed, of course; coal was no longer in demand, as it once was, and passenger revenues made up a growing part of the company's balance sheet. Plans were announced in 1947 to "modernize" the Reading Terminal with new ticket offices, waiting rooms, and escalators. The skylights in the shed were replaced with fireproof panels and the grand old wrought-iron gates at the entrances to the train platforms were removed. The Italian Renaissance look was out of fashion, and the arches on the Market Street façade were covered over with a massive concrete band meant to give the building a streamlined appearance. Much to the disappointment of the Reading brass, passenger numbers began to decline and the great hope for future revenues diminished. Reading began trying to economize, closing stations that were no longer needed and selling off real estate parcels. The company was also involved in labor disputes, and when a nationwide rail strike was threatened in 1950, the government took control of the rails for a time.

A Long, Slow Decline

The middle of the twentieth century was actually the end of a long period of prosperity for the market. Its annual reports from the 1950s depict a slow, nagging decline. In 1952, 98 percent of the stalls were occupied and the market made a profit, as did the cold-storage operation. By 1959 the market was 70 percent full and was running a deficit for the sixth straight year. The ice-making operation was discontinued in 1955. Real estate speculators were making offers to Reading to take over the market and turn it into a discount "Merchandise Mart." The city had approached the railroad about turning the market into a parking garage and bus terminal. Rumors that the market was up for sale raced through the stalls, and merchants were advised by Reading's real estate agent to "diversify or die."[12]

A group of four merchants—Charles Cristella, Henry Schmalenbach, William Margerum, and Joseph Juliana—and their attorney represented the Merchants Association at a meeting with Reading Company officials in 1958 to hear firsthand what was happening. They were told about the "precarious position of the railroads" and that though each and every operation of the company was under scrutiny, there was great concern about the continuing losses from the market and cold-storage operation. The merchants expressed interest in taking a long-term lease for the market and were told that "no deal would be consummated . . . without further giving the Merchants Association an opportunity to make a proposition which would be acceptable to Reading Company." Later, the merchants declined the sublease offer after admitting they didn't have the financial wherewithal or degree of cooperation within their membership.

It was not a good decade by any means. The last two original merchants, Franklin Field and John Seeds, who moved their wares across Filbert Street on a cold night in February 1892 from the old markets on Market Street, both died. The Reading Company announced a 16.5 percent rental increase for all merchants. The city opened a new food distribution center in South Philadelphia, convenient to highways and well outside the crowded city center. This was the death knell for the Dock Street Market, a place where many Reading Terminal Market tenants went to buy provisions for resale. Plans were made public for a new tunnel linking the Reading and Pennsylvania railroad lines, which would have a major negative impact on access and parking around the market. And on December 31, 1959, Reading announced that it would be closing the obsolete cold-storage operation, with one exception—Bassett's—which would be permitted to remain for five years and continue making ice cream.

The next decade began with another darkly foreboding incident. On the morning of January 16, 1960, a stray spark from a cutting torch in Reading's powerhouse located between Arch and Cherry Streets, just across from the market, caused a four-alarm fire, which shut down the tracks to the station and cut off power to the market. Aside from the loss of customers for the day, merchants' major concern was spoilage of perishable meats and produce, and they hastily brought in 50,000 pounds of dry ice that they packed into refrigeration units.

Even though business was slowly shifting downward, there was still a strong trade for many market tenants who served thousands of customers every week. It was important to keep up a good façade, in spite of the obstacles and the "suburban food palaces where housewives can get free cookies," as noted by Charles Cristella, the head of the Merchants Association at the time. Reading agreed to put part of the new rent increases into an advertising fund touting Reading Terminal Market as the place to get "everything to eat from venison to French shallots." A special Christmas promotion was planned featuring longtime female butcher and soprano Florence H. Yerger (whose stall was located where Harry G. Ochs & Sons is today), who entertained shoppers in the "chill air of the Reading Terminal Market" with her renditions of carols and "Ave Maria."[13] The singer accompanied herself on the piano as best she could, considering she had to wear gloves to keep warm.

The market still garnered favorable publicity, although articles were tinged with phrases like "a gloomy barn" and "once gleaming white tile counters are gray with dust and starting to crumble."[14] Some hopeful signs of new clientele with the redevelopment of the Society Hill area of the city were offset by the quiet departure of longtime tenants. By the mid-1960s occupancy had dropped to just over 50 percent. Market supporters were more nostalgic than enthusiastic. Even the little peculiarities, things that gave the market its texture and character, were disappearing, like the daily checker games at Iles Meats at the east end of Fourth Avenue. And most cruelly, in 1967 the *Philadelphia Inquirer* wrote, "Some day the Reading Terminal Market will go, and when the end does come it will be with great sadness."

It was like watching an old dog die. There was a feeling that little could be done, that the market had had its day and one day soon it would just roll over and not wake up again. No more bins of buckwheat flour, butchers in top hats, minced-ham sandwiches, goat's milk, Irish dulce, "barrel of turnips with each ticket to Chestnut Hill,"[15] old African American women from the Pine Barrens selling arbutus outside the market entrances, and no more damp sawdust floors.

Bankrupt Once Again

The Reading Company, the once mighty lord of the rails, gasped along. It too was deficit-ridden, close to bankruptcy (again), and threatening to shut down. The market's problems were the least of the company's worries. In fact, it saw the market as a potentially valuable piece of real estate that was underperforming and hired a real estate company to conduct a professional evaluation. The real estate firm's appraisal was clear: not only was the market (and the rest of the terminal) underperforming, but it also would be more valuable if it were torn down and redeveloped for some other use. No more long-term leases would be given to any market merchants; their future was short-term at best. The planned new railroad tunnel, still being touted as the Reading's next big project, would replace any need for the train shed, and the market was viewed as a gloomy, leaky, rat-infested barn that had outlived its usefulness. It was in the way of the future, just as the old sheds on High Street had once been.

The Reading Railroad again declared bankruptcy on November 23, 1971. As bad as that was, things could have been worse for the market if the railroad had remained solvent, for the Reading Company had been advised by one of the most vaunted real estate firms in the city to tear it down. Other threats loomed: the city's plans for Market Street East renewal called for replacing the terminal with commercial and office buildings. A good example of maximizing real estate value was right on the other side of City Hall, where the Pennsylvania Railroad's great shed was replaced with a complex of office buildings, plazas, and a skating rink.

The ensuing years brought little in the way of good news for the market or the railroad. One positive note, though, was the listing of the entire terminal on the National Register of Historic Sites and Places. The market, by appendage, was included in the designation, although some people thought that was taking things too far. "It is about as historic as an outhouse," said former Philadelphia commerce director Harry Bellinger in a comment published by the *Philadelphia Evening Bulletin.* Furthermore, he added, "The market continues to exist only by the winking and blinking of city officials" because of countless code violations.[16]

The trustees of the bankrupt Reading Railroad were responsible for overseeing the railroad's assets. They determined that the market was a money loser, and that Reading could no longer afford to operate it. There were plenty of lookers but no takers for the nearly two-acre market under the train shed. When someone finally offered fifty thousand a year to sublet the place, it was an easy decision, especially when weighed against terminating all the leases and closing the landmark. Sam Rappaport, a savvy real estate investor, had plans to turn the market into something akin to the recently renovated Faneuil Hall in Boston or Fisherman's Wharf in San Francisco. After negotiating with the trustees and pledging to spend five hundred thousand on improvements, he signed a five-year lease, beginning in 1976, with two five-year options.

Rappaport's attorney sent a letter to the remaining forty-seven merchants terminating their leases in thirty days and giving notice of an interim six-month lease with rents 50 percent to 100 percent higher. Tenants who refused to sign would be considered trespassers and would be "removed." New, longer-term leases were to be negotiated individually. All of the market's tenants had month-to-month leases, so there was little they could do. The stalwart merchants who had remained through troubled times were beginning to wonder if staying any longer was worthwhile.

Attorneys for the merchants filed a temporary restraining order and after consultation with the judge who was presiding over the Reading Railroad reorganization, Rappaport agreed to let the merchants remain in the market on a month-to-month basis. By July 1977 there were only thirty-five merchants remaining. The emptiness of the market was eerie; it was dimly lit and shabby. The merchants appealed in writing to Mayor Frank Rizzo, who had helped them before. The mayor sent his director of commerce to appeal to Rappaport to reassess the rent hikes, to no avail. As tenants continued to leave, customers' favorite counters went dark and many longtime supporters, who had come to the market for things they couldn't get elsewhere, stopped making the trip to Twelfth and Filbert.

After six months, Rappaport started tendering leases with increases of up to 200 percent and 400 percent, putting the squeeze on the last loyal merchants who refused to leave. Desperate, they again appealed to the Reading Company trustees and asked them to reconsider their earlier offer to sublease the market to the merchants when Rappaport's first five-year term expired. But in the same letter asking for help, the merchants also threatened to take legal action against the trustees, holding them as well as Rappaport accountable for the damage to the market.

The Reading Company, which had moved its headquarters from the terminal to a midrise, innocuous office building in the suburbs, instituted default proceedings against Rappaport in 1979. A settlement was reached that detailed, among other remedies, that Reading "buy out" Rappaport's $389,000 worth of "improvements" made to the market. The remaining term of the original lease and the two five-year options were terminated, and Reading was back in the market game.

During the early years of the railroad's bankruptcy, in 1973, a third of the Reading Company's shares had quietly been purchased by a group of prominent Chicago investors who calculated that the company's good assets, such as its enormous real estate portfolio—including thirteen acres in Center City Philadelphia—would be worth far more than the festering debris of asbestos claims, underground fires, and other wrecks left over from the glory days. Even before buying out Rappaport, the Reading Company was preparing to move its real estate division back to Twelfth and Market Streets to maximize the real estate assets. Trains still rolled in and out of the terminal but were now operated by the federally subsidized Conrail and Philadelphia's commuter rail system, Septa. Reading still owned the shed, the terminal, the market, the viaduct, and hundreds of miles of rights of way, as well as thousands of parcels of land scattered over its once vast domain.

Eighty-seven years had elapsed since 1893, when Reading triumphantly took up quarters at Twelfth and Market Streets. In 1980 the headhouse was eerie, largely abandoned, and pigeons flew in and out of broken windows as weeds rooted in cracks in the terra cotta. Rumbling trains filled the darkened hallways with ghostly sounds.

William R. Dimeling, a young lawyer-entrepreneur, was chosen to lead Reading's "new" real estate division. Much as Archibald Angus McLeod had done years earlier, Dimeling marched a team of young bucks into newly restored offices on the eighth floor of the terminal, overlooking the train shed. Cope Linder Architects, the firm that oversaw the restoration, liked the space and moved its own offices in on the Market Street side of the corridor. Cope Linder also designed some of the early innovations in the market, including the bright red light fixtures on the exterior and the monumental banners along Twelfth Street.

Reading decided to make a play with its substantial downtown Philadelphia real estate holdings. Proceeds from selling upstate railroad parcels would be used as fuel for the recharged operations of Reading's Eastern Real Estate Company. Dimeling and his charges had their orders and got to work.

The Stalwart Merchants

Downstairs, butcher Harry Ochs, whose father opened his business at the market in 1906, was the unofficial leader of the merchants, who were now down to a tight squadron of twenty-three, desperately hoping for a turnaround and mightily suspicious of a Reading that had abandoned them a few years before. The market was at its nadir, but it was still opening six days a week, still redolent of grandeur, and still drawing a grateful albeit dwindling base of patrons who couldn't do without their fix of the market "experience." Despite the bums who slept behind the walk-in refrigerated boxes, the stench of old blood and urine, the locked bathrooms, the leaks, and the broken windows, the market still had a decent flow of customers, and most of the remaining merchants were huddled in the southwestern quadrant so the market still had a sense of critical mass.

The biggest obstacle for the market at that time was the blockage of traffic, vehicular and pedestrian, caused by construction of the Center City commuter rail tunnel. Filbert Street and Twelfth Street were closed. The road, trolley tracks, and sidewalks were rerouted. Loyal customers, and loyal they were, had to wend a course of bridges, platforms, and temporary boardwalks to get into the market. Once they got inside, they had to be careful to avoid tripping over rodents and drunkards. The market was not a pretty sight.

Considering all that had gone against the merchants, it is hard to believe that there was even one left at this point. But the market was a way of life for them, and more than one merchant had died behind the counter, loyal to family, customer, and tradition. Yet even after Sam Rappaport was gone and Reading took over again, the holdouts were skeptical about another highfalutin comeback by the same Reading that had deserted the city, the market, and the trains.

Undaunted by a past they had nothing to do with, the new Reading upstarts embarked on a program to revive the market as a "super" market and started cleaning it up and looking for new tenants. A core group of young Amish families from Lancaster County saw opportunity in the mostly empty market, against the advice of some of their elders who visited and said they "didn't want any of their children in that place."[17] Suburban farmers' markets were doing well again, but potential merchants at those markets essentially had to buy out an existing tenant, while the startup costs at Reading Terminal Market were comparatively low—only utility hookup fees and equipment costs were needed to set up stalls. In 1980 the Amish took a chance and leased the large, vacant area at Twelfth and Arch Streets so they could set up together, and they began venturing in on Thursdays, Fridays, and Saturdays.

New immigrants from Korea, China, Lebanon, Holland, Turkey, Greece, Vietnam, Uganda, Peru, England, Switzerland, India, and Germany also liked the traditional atmosphere of the market and started opening up new businesses or buying out existing merchants, some preferring the cash flow of an ongoing operation. Nine-to-fivers who wanted their own businesses, disaffected merchants from the Italian Market on Ninth Street, and budding urban-food pioneers opened up stalls and rounded out the look of the emerging new Reading Terminal Market.

While new merchants moved in, old, abandoned walk-in boxes and rusted-out display cases were dismantled and removed. Many of the new curiosity seekers coming to the market were office workers who grabbed a quick lunch and watched the market parade from an open seating area that had been created in the middle of the market and fitted out with a vintage upright piano for good measure. The leases and rental systems were changed to allow for a dramatic increase in maintenance, promotions, and upkeep. Customers were reacquainted with the market through advertising, public relations, events, parties, and word-of-mouth.

Up-and-Coming

Center City was up-and-coming, and the "Society Hill effect" was rippling into new areas. Downtown was becoming an attractive place to live again. The market, as Benjamin Franklin had once remarked, was the "best of gardens,"[18] and city folk found that a visit there was the next best thing to either raising their own foodstuffs or running farther and farther out beyond the suburban ring to a farm stand. There were few supermarkets in the urban areas, so the door was wide open for Reading Terminal Market to become the central market for downtown.

A major push was on to promote the market as a food lover's paradise, with the finest merchants and farmers from the Delaware Valley and Lancaster County "[e]nsuring the market is second to none in quality and selection," as Dimeling envisioned.[19] There were still slow days, but a sea change was in the air. A few of the early new businesses failed, but most were succeeding and some expanded four and five times. Ro and Sons Produce, for instance, was well on its way to becoming the dominant fruit and vegetable purveyor in the city, overtaking a position long held by vendors in the Italian Market. The shift of customers coming back to the market was real, and the momentum was strong.

The long-neglected area around Reading Terminal Market was also seeing an upsurge in investment and speculation. Projects that could total a billion dollars over the next two decades were in the talking stages. Reading negotiated for development rights to the city's empty parcel at Eleventh and Market Streets in exchange for giving the city a permanent easement through the ground floor of the headhouse as the new entrance into the Market East Station of the nearly completed Center City commuter rail connection. Reading erected a 32-story office building on the site and also developed a 750-car parking garage that spanned Eleventh Street from Filbert to Arch to serve the needs of Reading Terminal Market and the Gallery shopping center.

Most ambitious of all, Reading was developing plans to take the lead in the largest construction project in the city, a new convention center. The city wanted to build a new facility to replace the aging Civic Center in West Philadelphia, and Reading proposed a massive, centrally located exhibit hall north of Arch Street that could be entered through the soon-to-be-empty train shed.

The buzz was back at the market. New tenants filled it to near capacity by 1984, capping the greatest period of growth since the market opened in 1892. Customers came in droves and welcomed back their old market. Increased business meant more rent, and more rental revenues allowed the Reading Company to make more investments in the market. Heat and air conditioning were added for the first time ever in 1986, the Filbert Street façade that had been closed and boarded up was restored, and four old entrances were reopened. Customer counts were totaling over ten thousand shoppers a day, and vendors' registers were ringing just like in the good old days.

The market was lauded in the local and national press and was visited by mayors from other cities who wanted a market for their citizens. Food festivals and cooking demonstrations featured leading chefs of the day, such as Julia Child and Alice Waters. The market was used for parties in the evening, and requests were granted to some folks who even wanted to get married there. The market had reclaimed its position as the central market for all people in the Philadelphia area, and the aisles heaved with rich, poor, old, young, vegetarians, carnivores, new immigrants, and stubborn diehards who never stopped coming in for their scrapple, buttermilk, and fresh-ground poppy seeds.

Reading Terminal Market was part of a national phenomenon: towns all across the country were starting new markets or fixing up old ones. Thousands of new outdoor farmers' markets were opening in parking lots, plazas, and streets from Palm Beach to Portland, Oregon. There was an untapped yearning for things made locally and for a place where patrons could support farmers and budding producers. The rediscovery of place and the appreciation of local culture that gives each community a special flavor were part of the energy that spurred the movement.

The market's reclaimed popularity put it in good stead for a looming showdown. Reading's proposed site, beginning at Twelfth and Market Streets and stretching north of Arch, was chosen by the city as the best place to build the new convention center. The Reading Company expected to be the private developer for the project, but this plan ultimately proved infeasible because the state was unwilling to put large amounts of public funding into what would have been a privately owned convention center. The effect on the market was unclear—and unsettling.

As plans progressed for the seven-acre convention center there was a lot of protesting, especially among the landlords and business owners in the center's "footprint," whose properties were to be condemned and razed. The fate of the market was always discussed and newspaper editorials pleaded for its protection, but no formal promises were made. When the Reading Company was put out of the developer's position and a state authority was formed to build and run the project, uncertainty and fear grew in the market.

Save the Market

The merchants took it upon themselves to build a case and affirm their interests. Bob Brecht, owner of the Coastal Cave Trading Company seafood business, was one of the savvy new breed of merchants who knew their way around a boardroom. He and Harry Ochs reenergized the Merchants Association and launched a sophisticated, grass-roots campaign to "save the market" once again. The merchants came together on this issue as strongly as their predecessors had when Archibald Angus McLeod announced his grand plans for the Reading Terminal, threatening the old markets nearly a century earlier.

The merchants' network was as wide and deep as anyone's in the city, and they put it to work. A core group of roll-up-your-sleeve vendors put in many hours handling the logistics of what would be a five-year effort. Petitions were posted on market counters, and in no time seventy thousand people had signed on demanding that the "Convention Center Authority change the construction of the convention center project so that it does not close the Market and its merchants temporarily or permanently." The merchants marched to City Hall, petitions in hand, and demanded protection for themselves and the institution. They hired a team of elite lawyers and began to craft their strategy.

Public support for the market was overwhelming, and no city politician dared get in the way. The newspapers saw the value of the market and editorialized again and again in favor of not only keeping the market physically, but also preserving its soul and its traditions. A blue-ribbon panel of high-profile Philadelphians was organized and added credibility to the campaign.

Meanwhile, the market kept up its day-to-day business, but that was anything but normal. The now empty train shed had to be cleared of pollutants before the Pennsylvania Convention Center would take title from the Reading Company. The remediation was slow, painstaking, loud, dirty work. Jackhammers overhead resounded through the market, making it difficult to hear customers and harder to think. The work caused many new leaks and big blue barrels were placed helter-skelter to catch rainwater, but they weren't much help. On bad days, and there were a lot of them, so much rain came into the market that virtual rivulets ran down the aisles and out the doors onto Twelfth Street; fish could have jumped off the counters and swum home. The management was told to close the market if necessary but never did, ever thankful that no one was hurt or electrocuted.

In short, there was no peace in the market. With negotiations running at full tilt, jackhammers shaking the foundations, and rainwater barrels blocking the aisles, everyone's nerves were frayed. Tempers flared even though everybody was fighting for the same cause.

The lawyers and merchants negotiated hard with the Convention Center Authority. After years of meetings, a comprehensive agreement was reached to keep the market open during construction of the Convention Center, and a fund was set up to pay merchants for losses attributable to the disruption. The Convention Center would rebuild the aging market from top to bottom and agreed to do so in a way that introduced a twenty-first-century infrastructure while keeping the historic stalls, marble counters, and a patina of finishes that had accumulated for more than a century.

After the Convention Center took control of the market in November 1990, the roof of the train shed was immediately rebuilt and by March 1991 the job was done, finally ending the leak problem. The complex plan for the reconstruction of the market was put into final form and executed in six stages, each lasting ten weeks, beginning in June 1992. This piecemeal approach was undertaken to ensure that the majority of the market would always remain open for business. As each section of the market was walled off and rebuilt, groups of tenants whose stalls were closed for reconstruction were temporarily relocated.

Today's Reading Terminal Market is as vibrant and colorful as ever. The market is still owned by the Pennsylvania Convention Center and is operated by a not-for-profit corporation set up specifically to run the historic market and preserve its character and historic role of bringing together local producers and consumers. The effect of the Convention Center is mixed; though it has brought more people into the market, they are people who buy lunch, not pork chops, beets, or provisions from Lancaster County. Some of the old purveyors have trickled out as more lunch stands have opened to cash in on the convention trade.

The future of the market will always bring an ever-changing course of new obstacles. But time has shown that there is no more agile institution in the city of Philadelphia. Anyone who has second-guessed the staying power of our market has been proved wrong for over one hundred years.

EARLY MARKETS

These two English markets illustrate the evolution of architectural style from simple covered stalls to a market with a town hall. The Chipping Campden market (top) was built in the 1400s and the Ross on Wye market (bottom) opened in 1670 in Wallingford. It became very common in England for the market and town hall to be combined in the same structure. The influence of this style was evident in eighteenth-century market houses in Philadelphia.

The first European-style market hall was built at Second and High Streets in 1708. This early market had civic offices upstairs, and the cupola housed a "butter bell" that was rung to signify the opening of the market or to warn the citizens if an enemy's boat was seen coming up the river.

These views inside the High Street sheds were published by W. Birch and Son in 1800. The original sheds were made of brick, but they were torn down in 1837 and replaced with new ones made of iron. The view on the top shows a commemorative parade held on the anniversary of George Washington's death on December 26, 1799.

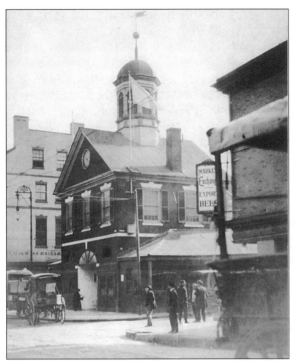

The first "suburban" market in Philadelphia was built in 1745 at Second and Pine Streets for southern residents of the growing city. At one time the New Market extended all the way to South Street. The market's style is very similar to that of the old Court House and Market at Second and High Streets. It has been modified many times over the years and was most recently restored in the 1970s. The market is still used occasionally on weekends for a crafts fair.

Another "Birch view" (from 1794) showing New Market, looking north from South Street toward Pine. The southern end of the market also had a headhouse, like the one that still stands on Pine Street. The sheds were made of brick piers, like the first generation of sheds on High Street.

This early photograph shows a butcher, Stockburger, displaying his freshly cut meat at New Market. Some vendors left this market and moved into Reading Terminal Market when it opened in 1892, lured, no doubt, by its state-of-the-art facilities and cold-storage area. Farmers have recently returned to sell in the open air on Second Street, adjacent to the old market, but have not been permitted to sell in the shed.

Similar to the town hall built at Second and High Streets, this smaller version in Northern Liberties at the intersection of Second and Coats Streets served as both a town hall and a market. The first floor was a small market house and covered sheds extended northward, providing additional selling space. The picture is from an original drawing by Benjamin Evans.   *Courtesy of the Library Company of Philadelphia.*

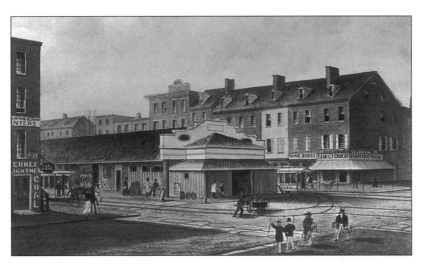

Typical of Philadelphia street markets, the Callowhill market was a series of sheds built in the middle of the street. At its height, the Callowhill Street Market stretched all the way to Seventh Street. This view is from the southeast corner of Seventh and Callowhill.   *Courtesy of the Library Company of Philadelphia.*

This fancy shed for the Philadelphia Fish Market was built in 1816 on High Street, east of Water Street. The market was considered an "ornament to the city," and the gable on the east end of the shed was decorated with a beautifully carved shad. The placement of the fish market close to the wharves on the Delaware River was no accident; this location made it easy to unload fresh catches and take them right into the market. It was demolished in 1859.

The foot of Market Street where the old Fish Market stood has changed many times over the years. This view, showing the Pennsylvania Railroad's ferry terminal, is from about 1910.

The shed on the 500 block of High Street was first built in 1810 and rebuilt in 1837. The rebuilt version (shown) was made narrower to allow for the passage of railcars from a branch of the Philadelphia and Columbia Railroad that ran between the shed and the sidewalk. Trains were permitted to travel at only three miles per hour on High Street, and never on market days.   *Reprinted from Jackson,* Market Street, *p. 109. Collection of author.*

This lithograph dramatizes an 1830 view up High Street and shows, in order, the Fish Market at the wharves, the Jersey Market at Water Street, and the old State House and market building at Second Street. Notice how steep the first few blocks of High Street were and that the State House was the natural high point for the city.

Second and Market Streets, the intersection just above the trolleys in this 1906 photograph, was the highest point in the early city and site of the old State House and market sheds that ran west up the middle of the street. This view is lost today, because of I-95, which cut the city off from the Delaware River.

OTHER MARKETS AND FOOD TRANSPORT

One of the first of the market halls to be built, Eastern Market was on the southeast corner of Fifth and Merchant Streets, below High Street, where the Bourse Building stands today. The market was known for its lavish use of glass windows. This photograph was taken in November 1859 at the dinner marking the opening of the market. Top hats and white aprons were the appropriate attire for the occasion. *Courtesy of the Library Company of Philadelphia.*

Photo of the Eastern Market's exterior. The market had 148 feet of frontage on Fifth Street and extended 400 feet east to Fourth Street. The market was demolished in the 1890s.

Before a new food distribution center opened in 1959, the Dock Street area was one of the principal wholesale markets in Philadelphia. Many Reading Terminal Market merchants bought products here and took them to Twelfth and Filbert Streets for resale. The Dock Street Market was largely removed in the 1960s, although the cobblestone-paved street was preserved.

Philadelphia has always loved markets of all kinds, and outdoor markets have a special appeal. Rarely seen today, street markets such as this "famous" flower market were once common.

The Ridge Avenue Farmers Market (at Eighteenth Street and Ridge Avenue) opened in 1875 and was torn down in 1997. The market was built and financed by the stallholders, as were most of the markets built in the last half of the nineteenth century in Philadelphia. The original market included stables and a hotel.

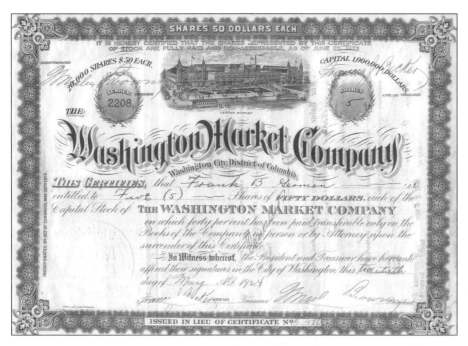

Center Market, also known as Washington Market, in Washington, D. C., was established by an Act of Congress in 1870 and opened in 1877. Shares in the market, as shown by this stock certificate, were sold to finance its construction. The market was nicknamed the Marsh Market because of its frequent flooding by the Potomac (Algonquin for "trading place") River. George McKay, Reading Terminal Market's first and longest-serving superintendent, was hired away from Center Market after being offered nearly twice the salary he was making and the chance to open the greatest market in the United States. The Center Market was torn down in the 1920s, and the site at Seventh and Pennsylvania Avenues is now the home of the National Archives Building.

A perspective of the rear of the Center Market on a busy morning. The sign above the doors on the right side of the photograph says *Dining Rooms*.

Ferryboats were an important form of transport to bring New Jersey farm goods to markets in Philadelphia. Penn's Grove, where this ferry was docked, is located in New Jersey, south of Philadelphia on the Delaware River. The sacks ready to be loaded on the ferry *Ulrica* are labeled *Lea Bran*.

The growth of a national train network made it possible to ship citrus fruit from farms in Florida to markets in the north.

FARMERS' AND TWELFTH STREET MARKETS

The Farmers' Market opened in 1860, before the Twelfth Street Market was built. In this photograph you can see that the site next to the Farmers' Market is still empty, although it has been cleared. Notice the boxcar moving up Market Street.

Reading Terminal Market's predecessors operated side by side for many years. The Farmers' Market was the larger of the two and opened first. The Twelfth Street Market was originally called the Franklin Market and first opened on South Tenth Street between Chestnut and Market. A statue of the market's namesake, mounted above the main market door, was removed and can be seen today in the lobby of the Public Ledger Building at Sixth and Chestnut Streets. Both of the markets in the photograph were demolished in 1892.   *Courtesy of the Library Company of Philadelphia.*

Built in 1860 on land purchased from the Pennsylvania Railroad, the Farmers' Market was the largest market in the city. It was incorporated and owned by farmers. It was normally open on Wednesdays and Saturdays when the farmers, mostly from outlying counties, brought in their products. The market even had sleeping quarters on an upper floor on the Filbert Street end of the building. The market was condemned to make way for Reading's new terminus, but eventually a $600,000 settlement was reached and many of the farmers moved into the new Reading Terminal Market on February 22, 1892.   *Reprinted from Strahan,* A Century After, *p.156.*

The Twelfth Street Market as it looked just before demolition in 1892, in a drawing that appeared in the *Philadelphia Record* newspaper. The market was built in the early 1860s and was also called the New Franklin Market.   *Courtesy of* Philadelphia Record.

Headline on the front page of the *Philadelphia Record* on February 14, 1892. Contractor Charles McCaul was in charge of the demolition of the old markets and of building the new terminal.   *Courtesy of* Philadelphia Record.

READING TERMINAL MARKET

These 1891 images show construction crews clearing the site between Filbert and Arch Streets for the Reading train shed and market. The rear of the Twelfth Street and Farmers' Markets are visible on the left sides of the pictures. City Hall was under construction, and in the background of the picture on the bottom the tower can be seen taking shape and rising up above its surroundings.

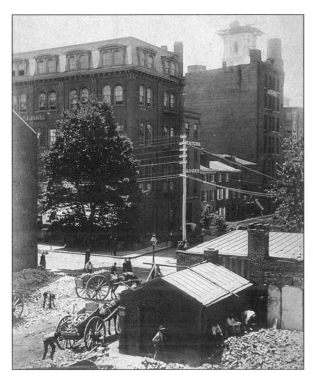

Another view from Twelfth and Filbert Streets shows the demolition activity under way to clear space for the Reading Terminal. *Courtesy of the Library Company of Philadelphia.*

The *Philadelphia Record* depicted the first arch of the train shed (looking north from Twelfth and Filbert Streets) being erected over the nearly completed Reading Terminal Market. This section of the terminal was finished before construction began on the headhouse. *Courtesy of Philadelphia Record.*

This view, looking south toward Arch Street, probably dates from early 1892 and shows construction of the terminal well under way. In the foreground, amid all the debris, well-dressed men in top hats are looking down the large hole of the excavation, next to a stepped pile of granite, which is part of the foundation. It also appears that the two old market houses have been torn down south of the shed, as it is possible to see all the way to Snellenburg's Department Store on Market Street.

This commemorative postcard was issued in 1898 and shows the full perspective of the headhouse, shed, and market. At this time, there were two through streets that ran under the terminal. Filbert Street is still open and Hunter Street, just south of Filbert and now closed, was used for freight and mail deliveries.

The canopy and the clock seen in front of the Reading Terminal in this 1905 photograph were both added as an afterthought, to dress up the building and make it more commuter-friendly. Snellenburg's, directly across Market Street, was a major shopping destination. In 1817 the same site was briefly the home of Joseph Bonaparte, former King of Spain.

In 1906 the only visible change since the previous year was the canopy added in front of the Hotel Vendig, which stood on the northwest corner of Twelfth and Market Streets. The hotel remained there until it was torn down for the new Marriott that was built to service the Convention Center. The roadways in 1906 were still shared by horses and streetcars.

The Reading Terminal and shed dominated the early-twentieth-century skyline on east Market Street.

The Reading Terminal is featured in the photograph inset at the upper right of this postcard.

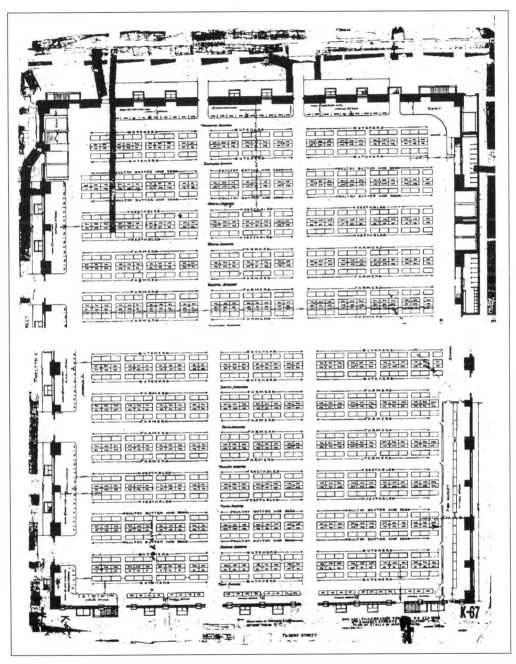

Complete floor plan of Reading Terminal Market drawn January 14, 1891, by the engineering firm Wilson Brothers. The market has twelve east-west aisles and four north-south aisles. There were eight elevators along the eastern and western walls that went from the basement cold-storage area to the market to the train shed. The old stairwells and loading chutes on the exterior of the building have all been paved over and are no longer used.   *Courtesy of the Athenaeum of Philadelphia.*

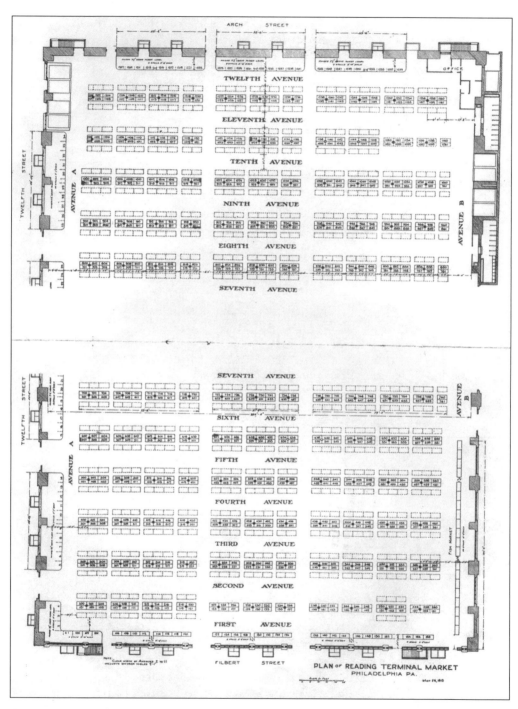

A 1913 version of the market's floor plan is almost identical to the original.

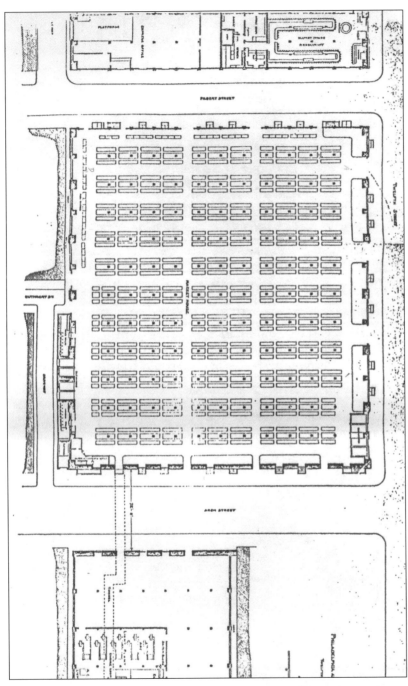

This drawing shows the market in relation to the terminal across Filbert Street and to the powerhouse across Arch Street.

This drawing depicts the interior of the unfinished market. The sturdy column grid ensured that the trains would be properly supported above the new market, which operated for several years without a ceiling and was plagued with leaks.
Courtesy of Philadelphia Record.

Archibald Angus McLeod, president of the Reading Company during the planning and construction of the new terminal on Twelfth Street, was often involved in the smallest details of the market, all the while completing some of the largest deals in the history of American industry. McLeod, a native of Canada, was himself a former trainman. His tenure in the top position lasted only a short period, from 1890 until the Reading declared bankruptcy in 1893.
Courtesy of Hagley Museum and Library.

This editorial cartoon in which the Pennsylvania Railroad is poking fun at Archibald Angus McLeod and the Reading for having a market in its station gives a glimpse into nineteenth-century humor. One of the banners flying on the roof reads *Our fish are fresh, our officials and employees are not*. The once belittled market has outlasted both of the mighty railroads.

George H. McKay, the first superintendent of Reading Terminal Market, started on the job January 1, 1892. He had been working at the Center Market in Washington, D.C. *Courtesy of Mary Holmes.*

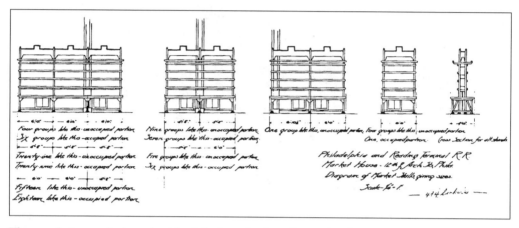

The market was designed with eight hundred stalls made of iron and wood. The stalls ranged in width from five feet eight inches to six feet ten inches and were built to stand alone or in groupings of two or three. The stallholder's name was placed in the upper section and each stall was numbered much like houses on a street, with odd numbers on one side of the market aisle and even numbers on the other. This is a diagram of some market stalls.   *Courtesy of the Athenaeum of Philadelphia.*

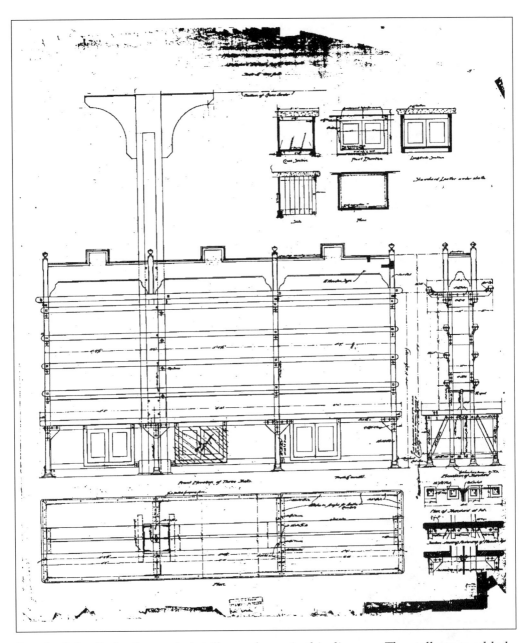

Standard details for the market stalls are shown in this diagram. The stalls were added shortly after the market opened, and many are still in use today. Wooden crossbars held iron hooks for hanging products and under-counter cabinets provided a modicum of storage.   *Courtesy of the Athenaeum of Philadelphia.*

This photo of the market's Avenue D looking toward Filbert Street shows an early view of the fish stalls. The thick marble counters were specially designed to display fish and sloped to carry melting ice into built-in drain lines.   *Courtesy of the Historical Society of Pennsylvania.*

Edwin T. McKay (also known as Nash) was born in Deer Isle, Maine, in 1857 and followed his older brother, George, to Philadelphia to oversee the cold-storage area of the market.   *Courtesy of Mary Holmes.*

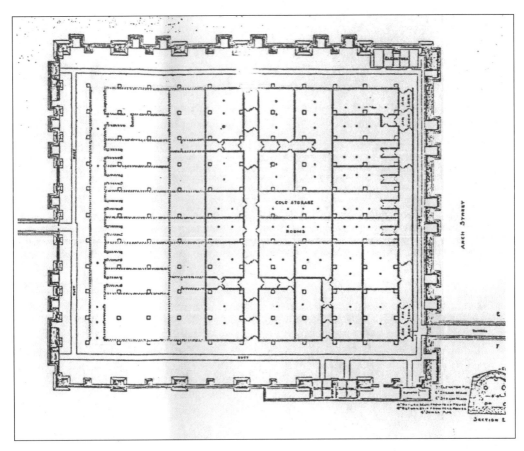

Diagram of market basement showing cold- and dry-storage rooms.

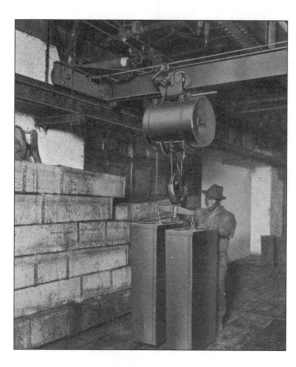

Taken in 1923, this view of the Reading Terminal Market and Cold Storage Company's ice plant shows an employee in the tank room, which was located on the north side of Arch Street. The two cans under the hoist held cakes of ice. The ice plant made nearly a ton of ice every hour, twenty-four hours a day, and was capable of storing up to seventy-five hundred cakes (each weighing three hundred pounds) to supply the needs of the market, the railroad, and outlying stations.

As general superintendent of the Philadelphia and Reading Railway Company in the early part of the twentieth century, Agnew T. Dice was responsible for the entire terminal and oversaw expansion of the cold-storage area and decades of prosperity in the market.

Ferd. W. Nofer was one of the market's original stallholders. Prior to setting up shop at Reading Terminal Market, Nofer sold meats at a stall in "New Market" at Second and Pine Streets.

Ferd. W. Nofer's business in the northeast corner of Reading Terminal Market specialized in wholesale and retail meats. The business moved out of the terminal in the 1970s.

Bassett's Ice Cream was selling from a storefront (second from right) on Market Street in the 1870s. The business, which was started in 1861, moved to the Twelfth Street Market in 1882. The Bassett family was among the original stallholders in Reading Terminal Market in 1892.   *Courtesy of Bassett's Ice Cream.*

Formal portrait of Louis Dubois Bassett, patriarch and founder of Bassett's Ice Cream. Bassett was a Quaker schoolteacher from Salem, New Jersey, and started churning ice cream in his backyard.   *Courtesy of Bassett's Ice Cream.*

TELEPHONE 2305.

John Haag

⁞ BUTTER ⁞
ᴀɴᴅ EGGS

Stalls 5, 6, 7, 8, 9, 10 Avenue A,

AND

400, 402, 404, 406 Fourth Avenue,

READING TERMINAL MARKET

Twelfth Street, Filbert to Arch.

Advertisement of farmer/vendor John Haag, one of the original Reading Terminal Market vendors from 1892. Haag had six large stalls in a prime location next to the entrance at Twelfth and Filbert Streets along the Twelfth Street wall (where Pearl's Oyster Bar is today). Stalls along the perimeter walls are deeper than stalls along numbered avenues.

An exquisite turn-of-the-century market display at one of the stalls owned by William B. Margerum, who got his start in 1876 in the Twelfth Street Market and was one of the original tenants of Reading Terminal Market. His family operated a business there until 2001.

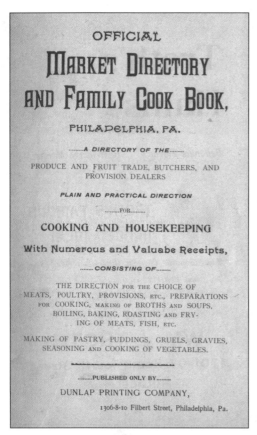

The first market cookbook, published in 1900, was 125 pages full of tips on how to buy, store, and cook all manner of foodstuffs. It is amusing to see how tastes have changed in terms of vocabulary choices as well as ingredients.

This is the latest Reading Terminal Market cookbook, published by Camino Books in 1997.

The first engine to enter the train shed was Engine 159, which arrived on Track 1 in 1892, before the official opening of the shed in 1893.   *Reprinted from* Reading Railroad *Magazine 12, nos. 10–11 (March–April 1948).*

The terminal had its own post office for years, and Reading had contracts to carry the U.S. Mail. The mail was sent down chutes to the post office at street level. The trains also carried many packages for the market, sending baskets to outlying stations, where customers would pick them up.

George F. Baer was president of the Philadelphia and Reading Railway Company from 1901 to 1914, when he died walking to his office in the Reading Terminal. He was succeeded by Edward T. Stotesbury.

J.C. Wyman's Market House was a landmark restaurant that opened in the terminal in 1893 on the south side of Filbert Street, across from the market. Originally called Partridge's, it was opened by a restaurateur from the old Twelfth Street Market. The place was a favorite of market merchants and farmers as well as commuters and office workers.

The area around the market was a hub for restaurants. The interior of the famous "Old Venice" at Twelfth and Filbert Streets is interesting for the tile work and combination of table and counter seating.

As is true today, there were many hotels in the area surrounding the market. The Hanover was located on the northwest corner of Twelfth and Arch Streets. In the 1920s, the hotel advertised rooms with hot and cold running water in every room at a daily rate of one dollar and up.

The Hotel Windsor, on Filbert Street between Twelfth and Thirteenth Streets, was on the middle of the block now occupied by a large parking garage. The train shed is visible in the background with a large sign saying *Reading Terminal* on the roof. The view down Filbert Street would have been a prime sight corridor from the rival Pennsylvania Station, just three blocks west.

Felix Spatola left Calabritto, Italy, in the 1880s for Philadelphia. Starting with a basket of lemons he purchased at the Dock Street Market, Spatola soon opened in Reading Terminal Market in the choice Twelfth and Filbert Street corner shown in this photograph from 1905. He built the business into a large wholesale and retail operation serving many hotels, restaurants, and institutions throughout the city. *Courtesy of the Historical Society of Pennsylvania.*

Harry Ochs Sr. opened his butcher business at Reading Terminal Market in 1906. The business continues to flourish today as Harry Jr. operates it with his two sons, Harry III and Nicholas. Considered by many to be the finest butchers in the city, the Ochs family has served generations of customers. Harry Ochs Jr. ably guided the Merchants Association through many struggles and fought hard to save the market from being closed during the construction of the Convention Center.

William Groff Ziegler left the Spring Garden Farmers Market and went to Reading Terminal Market shortly after it opened. Initially the family members working the stall would drive a horse and wagon from their home in Schwenksville, Montgomery County, and spend the night in the city at a hotel near the market. Later on, they took everything in by train. Bill Ziegler, who started working at the market in 1927, remembers the 1956 transition from ice to refrigeration to keep things cool at the stalls on the market floor. The family had its own farm, slaughterhouse, and butcher shop in Perry County. Ziegler's did a big wholesale business selling to butchers throughout Philadelphia and also rented cold-storage space in the market's basement. Ziegler's sold at the market until 1970. This picture was taken looking west down Eighth Avenue. Left to right: Hasting Ziegler, Elsie Ziegler, Harrison Ziegler, Betsy Ziegler, Ed Bolden, and Hulda Ziegler.   *Courtesy of William Ziegler.*

This 1907 view shows the many ways people traveled to the market: by train, horse, streetcar, automobile, truck, and on foot. The old photo has many interesting period details such as cobblestone streets, steam plumes in the train shed, and transom windows along the Twelfth Street façade of the market.

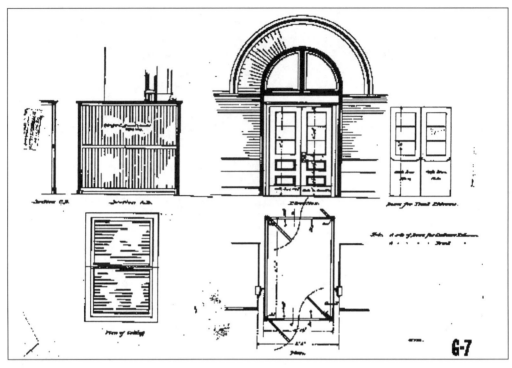

This drawing shows details of the doors on Arch Street. Those doors are arched, unlike all the other entrances, which are rectangular. The market originally had twelve entrances plus service entrances on the east side of the market building. *Courtesy of the Athenaeum of Philadelphia.*

This 1917 photo of the corner of Twelfth and Arch Streets documents several interesting features. The sign on the Arch Street wall says *Have your purchases sent home on the Terminal Market Delivery Cars.* Skylights are visible in the train shed. Today, the stairwell on the corner has been discontinued and paved over, and all of the entrances have storm door additions. *Courtesy of the Library Company of Philadelphia.*

Cover of a souvenir directory published by the market in 1913 that contained pictures of vendors, advertisements, and telephone numbers.

Markets attract a subculture of knife sharpeners, bag sellers, foragers, and "micro entrepreneurs" who don't even require a stall to set up shop. There was a tradition, in the markets of days gone by, in which older women would sell pepper pot soup to hungry shoppers for a quick pick-me-up. *Reprinted from Strahan,* A Century After, *p. 165.*

The telephone on the counter in this 1907 view of Margerum's shows one of the first phones used at the market. Much of the early business at the market was called in and then sent out in baskets.   *Courtesy of Noelle Margerum.*

Margerum's did a tremendous business over the phone and shipped orders all over the country.   *Courtesy of Noelle Margerum.*

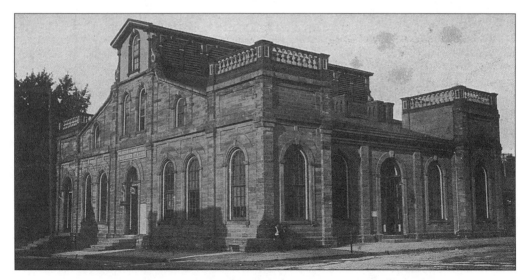

The railroad depot in Chestnut Hill was one of the many outlying stations on the Reading system where customers could have their orders shipped from Reading Terminal Market. This picture was taken about 1906.

Strode's was one of the market's original tenants and was famous for scrapple and sausages from the family's farm in Chester County. The Strode family operated in the market until the mid-1980s when they sold the business. The baskets hanging from the meat hooks in this picture were filled with market products and sent out on the trains.

William Evans was a longtime fish vendor in the market and at one time had over fifty stalls in the market's southeast corner, which was the fish section of the market. Evans had thirty-five employees and five trucks and sold both wholesale and retail. He also operated an oyster bar on the east wall of the market, which can be seen in the photo on the bottom. His business was purchased by William Harley, who was the last fish vendor in this corner of the market and closed in 1980.

A view looking past Franklin Field's toward Evans Seafood around 1920. Field's stalls were on Second Avenue between Avenues C and D, in the east end of the market. *Courtesy of Harvey Reilly.*

Franklin Field had a small farm on Red Lion Road at the Roosevelt Boulevard in Northeast Philadelphia where he grew many of the herbs and vegetables for his market stall. Fred Cannon worked on the farm and helped out at the market. The site of the farm is now a nursing home.   *Courtesy of Harvey Reilly.*

Franklin Field supplied Wanamaker's department store with coconut for all of the store's cakes and desserts. The coconut was ground fresh daily in the market. As both of these photographs show, drying coconuts hang from above, waiting to be cracked with an axe.   *Courtesy of Harvey Reilly.*

The north-south aisles are numbered one to twelve and the four east-west aisles are lettered A, B, C, and D. Each intersection in the market had one of these directional signs that made it easy to find a particular stall. The stall numbers and aisle signs are used little today, and customers seem to enjoy asking for directions or just exploring on their own. Signs like this were made in the 1930's.

This photograph shows the market aisles full of products. One of the old superintendents used to take a measuring stick around the market and measure encroachments. The nine-foot-wide aisles are just wide enough for market traffic and a few display barrels here and there for extra atmosphere.   *Courtesy of Harvey Reilly.*

The Merchants Association produced an annual series of promotions beginning in 1931. This is the official program cover for the show in 1934. The eight-day promotion featured an orchestra, a cooking school, and exhibits.

Employee Rick Braun stands behind an old wooden hatch on top of the counter at Frankenfield's Poultry (formerly Godshall's). Before the advent of refrigerated display cases, the hatch was lifted and ice was placed below the counters to keep products cold. *Courtesy of Anne Day.*

New entrances and refrigerated windows were installed on Twelfth Street in 1934 as part of the first major renovation of the market since it opened.

Close-up of a new refrigerated window installed in 1934. Large displays of fruit and produce were artfully presented to tempt shoppers and give a hint of the bounty to be found inside the market.

It is not unusual to see displays of humor at the market. This fellow was known to show up for work every now and then at Pierce and Schurr Meats.

The Moyers' farm business began in 1865 in Perkasie, Montgomery County, and the family started selling at the market in 1904. Before they had a truck, they would take a horse and wagon to the Perkasie train station and ride all the way in to the Reading Terminal, where they would transfer their products into the market by elevator from the train floor. Various branches of the Moyer family sold in the market until 1997. This 1948 family portrait shows, left to right: Ruth Moyer, Ed Wimmer, Wallace Moyer, Alice Moyer, and Robert Moyer.   *Courtesy of Bob Moyer.*

This photograph of the Moyer family's farm in Perkasie shows young Moyer children playing in the chicken yard in 1907.

Eugene and Alice Moyer specialized in a wide range of fresh farm products at stalls 935 and 937. The appearance of these stalls has changed little over the years. This photograph was taken in 1929.
Courtesy of Bob Moyer.

Ernie Godshall's father moved his poultry business into Reading Terminal Market in 1916 from the old Oxford Market (Twentieth and Oxford Streets) that was popular with many farmers from Montgomery County. Like many other upcountry farmers, Ernie's father took his market goods in by train from the Hatfield Station to the Reading Terminal until 1930, when he switched over to a truck. This photograph of Ernie Godshall was taken in the 1940s.   *Courtesy of Ernie Godshall.*

Wallace Derstein was a farmer from Hatfield, Montgomery County, and was also Ernie Godshall's uncle. Derstein sold his goods from stalls 538, 540, and 542, where Coastal Cave Trading Company is today. It was quite common for different stallholders to be related, and also not uncommon for couples who eventually married to have met in Reading Terminal Market.   *Courtesy of Ernie Godshall.*

Ernie Godshall married Eva Halteman, a member of another prominent Reading Terminal Market family, in 1941. Eva Halteman's brother, Lester, ran a farm stand just up Fourth Avenue for many years.   *Courtesy of Ernie Godshall.*

Lester Halteman took over a longstanding market business from his father. Lester, himself a farmer from Montgomery County, sold at the market until the 1990s, when he sold his business to Mennonite neighbors who continue the tradition of bringing farm-fresh produce and poultry to market. They still carry Halteman's prized Muscovy ducks. *Courtesy of Ernie Godshall.*

Dominic Spataro started selling his generously proportioned sandwiches and buttermilk at the market in 1947. Back then buttermilk was considered fortifying—and after enjoying a glass with one of Spataro's famous sandwiches, customers probably didn't need to have any dinner. The old counter was a favorite meeting place for market regulars who still flock to Spataro's new location across the aisle. The sign with the slogan "Drink buttermilk, live longer" is still there and can be seen if you look up. *Courtesy of Anne Day.*

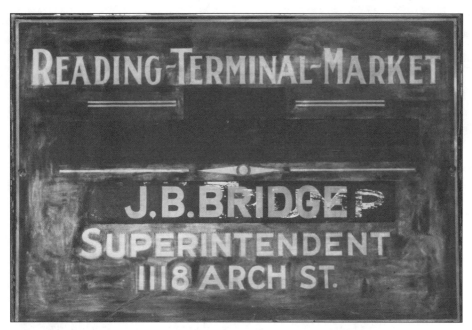

This sign hung above the superintendent's office in the northeast corner of the market. J. B. Bridge was superintendent from the late 1950s to the late 1960s. The painted-out area under *Reading Terminal Market* used to say *and Cold Storage* until that area was closed in 1960.

Members of the Margerum family stand for a picture outside the market. For many years Margerum's was the largest merchant in the market and the largest meat purveyor in the city. Left to right: Charles H. Margerum Sr., William Brown Margerum, and Edwin Patten Margerum.   *Courtesy of Noelle Margerum.*

John Seeds, on the left, and Franklin Field, on the right, two of the market's original tenants, discuss the day's business in the 1950s. Seeds sold butter and eggs, and Field sold produce and orchids and was famous for his freshly ground coconut, peanut butter, and poppy seed. *Courtesy of Harvey Reilly.*

Franklin Field and John Seeds in front of Supiot's at the intersection of Avenue A and Sixth Avenue, where Kamal's Middle Eastern Specialties now operates. Supiot's was known for its selection of herbs and exotic produce.   *Courtesy of Harvey Reilly.*

The Lengles were an old market family from Line Lexington, Bucks County, that sold at the Ridge Avenue Farmers Market (Eighteenth Street and Ridge Avenue) and Reading Terminal Market. They occupied stalls where Salumeria now operates on Third Avenue. This is a photograph of Ralph Lengle, an old market vendor. *Courtesy of Harvey Reilly.*

In this photograph from the early 1960s, the grandeur of the market shows signs of fading. The once abundant stalls were going vacant and old-time merchants were just hanging on. Market occupancy dropped below 70 percent in 1960 and continued to slide for another twenty years.   *Courtesy of Harvey Reilly.*

The "center" of the market was nothing more than abandoned stalls in the late 1970s. This view looking down Sixth Avenue toward Bassett's Ice Cream shows what is now the market's central seating area, which is also used regularly for festivals, parties, musicians, temporary vendors, and special events.

The basement was closed in 1960 and abandoned for twenty years. The once sanitary space became eerie, filled with cobwebs and stagnant pools. Reading gutted the space as part of its renovation in the 1980s. It is once again being used for market storage.

This picture of the original fish section was taken looking down Avenue D toward the southeast entrance, closest to Eleventh and Filbert Streets. Avenue D has the highest elevation in the market (closest to and parallel with Eleventh Street), which provided better drainage for the mass quantities of water used at the fish counters.

This 1980 view shows the old stalls, still solid and standing after almost ninety years. The old stalls in the market today are to be preserved for posterity and may not be removed.

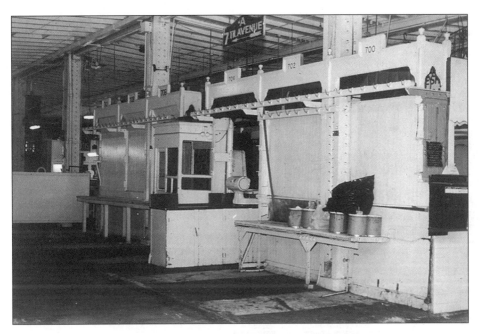

Another view of the abandoned market stalls.

The northeast corner of the market was nearly empty in 1980 except for a few walk-in boxes. This is now a lively and colorful corner, with businesses such as the popular Pennsylvania General Store and Foster's Gourmet Cookware.

Taken in 1980, this photo shows the strong-willed band of merchants that remained when the Reading Company took the market back from Sam Rappaport.   *Courtesy of Bruce A. Blank, © 1980.*

The northwest corner of the market as it appeared in 1980 just before a group of Amish merchants moved in and set up stalls.

The variety of fresh, local products at the market is one of its greatest attractions. Each egg is inspected by hand before being placed in a box and tied with string, just like in the "good old days."   *Courtesy of Burk Uzzle.*

The continued presence of the Amish merchant families is another reminder that Reading Terminal Market has strong ties to the region's culture.   *Courtesy of Burk Uzzle.*

This is a cleaned-up view of what was to become the central seating area in 1981. Once the basement cold-storage area closed in 1960 many stallholders built cold-storage boxes on the market floor. The placement of the boxes eventually created a walling effect, closing off much of the market. Removal of the boxes opened up large areas for new uses.

The central courtyard area was created in anticipation of the rise in demand for ready-to-eat foods. Many of the market's new customers were introduced to the market as a place for a fast and friendly lunch and, after seeing the variety of fresh foods, became shoppers as well.   *Courtesy of Burk Uzzle.*

New banners hang from the side of the train shed to announce the positive changes taking place inside the market in 1980. The "23" trolley still ran its route from Chestnut Hill to Tenth and Bigler Streets, passing Reading Terminal Market on every run. The old neighborhood had quite a few notable restaurants, including Kelly's, which was famous for oysters.

The reviving market became a favored venue for after-hours parties in the early 1980s. The Fabric Workshop, which for many years was located at 1133 Arch Street, hosted a festive black-tie fundraiser in the market with an orchestra, dancing, and dinner. This photograph shows the central seating area and the old market upright piano. The banners hanging from the ceiling were designed by artists from around the world and produced in the studios of the Fabric Workshop. This party was the first to be held in the market in decades. The market is still in vogue as a party destination to this day.

In 1980, the movie *Trading Places* starring Eddie Murphy used Reading Terminal Market for some of its scenes.

Pearl's Oyster Bar originally opened along the Arch Street wall and subsequently moved to Avenue A. Pearl's features excellent seafood platters and world-famous snapper soup made fresh from scratch by talented chef Robert Swinton.
Courtesy of Burk Uzzle.

This picture was taken looking north on Avenue A in 1980. Pearl's Oyster Bar is in the foreground and Bassett's Ice Cream is farther down the aisle on the left.

This series of still photographs was excerpted from a Bassett's Ice Cream Company video. Bassett's, established in 1861, made all of its ice cream in the basement of Reading Terminal Market beginning in 1898. Using milk from prize Guernsey cows, the cream was separated, cooled, and trucked to the market, where it was pasteurized, homogenized, and further cooled to thirty-eight degrees. The first picture shows the ice cream, made fresh daily, being drawn from the thickening machine and tested for air.

The next picture (bottom, facing page) shows the ice cream, now in cans, being placed in the hardening cabinet (full of salt and ice) for four hours to lower the temperature and "set" the product. The third shot (top) shows the can being delivered to the counter upstairs (see man in lower left with back to camera) ready for sale to eager customers. The fourth picture shows the band saw in the stall that was used to cut dry ice for packing ice cream to go.   *Courtesy of Bassett's Ice Cream.*

Longtime market butcher Bill Notis held court at his stall (where Spataro's now operates) in 1981, talking with Reading Company executive Steve Park about plans to restore the market.

Steve Frankenfield, nephew of Ernie and Eva Godshall, poses with them at the old stalls (455 and 457) where he learned the ropes before taking over the business in the 1980s. Steve has since moved across the aisle and has a much larger stand, but he continues the tradition of quality and country goodness that generations of customers have come to expect. Ernie still comes into the market once a week to help out and greet longtime market friends.   *Courtesy of Ernie Godshall.*

Reading Company President John Sullivan, on the right, and Philadelphia's Mayor Bill Green, on the left, cut a railroad-inspired cake in the central seating area to celebrate the market's ninetieth birthday. Free cake was given to thousands who came for the festivities. The celebration included Mummers, a twelve-hundred-foot flag, and farm animals.

Traffic on Twelfth Street was rerouted during the last phases of the commuter rail tunnel construction in the early 1980s. The massive project caused seemingly interminable disruption for normal pedestrian and vehicular traffic to Reading Terminal Market.

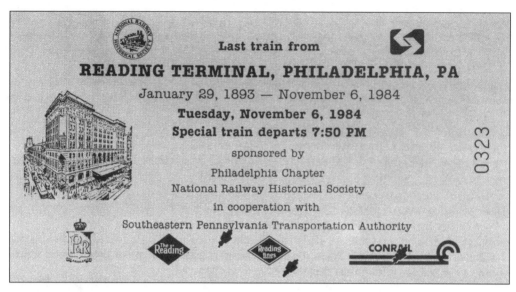

The last train left the Reading Terminal on November 6, 1984. Trains were rerouted into the new underground commuter tunnel linking the Reading and Pennsylvania commuter lines.

Button given out by SEPTA on November 6, 1984, the day the last train left the Reading Terminal. The next day, all trains were rerouted into the new center city commuter rail connection, which still stops at Twelfth and Market Streets, but underground. The station is called Market East.

The Reading Company built a 750-car parking garage on the east side of the terminal in 1983 for the market and the Gallery mall. The foundation for the garage was engineered to bear the load of a high-rise office building or hotel. A Hilton hotel was built on top of the garage after the Convention Center opened.

The market installed heat and air conditioning in 1986 as part of a larger renovation project and gave out commemorative fans as part of the celebration. The project gave the market climate control after ninety-four years of operating in the heat and the cold.

Herman Cherry worked on the market staff for many years and was the unofficial ambassador for the place. He was a great cheerleader for all of the market businesses. One of his favorite expressions was "Pile it high and watch it fly."

Isaac "Ike" Salter holds the ladder for Earl McLeod as he replaces light bulbs in the Twelfth Street fixtures. Ike worked on the maintenance crew for Reading's Eastern Real Estate Company and Earl was the longtime facilities manager for Reading Terminal Market, taking care of everything from operating the new heating and air-conditioning system to overseeing the construction of over sixty new businesses that opened in the 1980s.

Kyu Chang Ro emigrated from Korea to the United States in the 1970s and opened a stall at Reading Terminal Market in 1980, building one of the largest retail fruit and vegetable operations in the area. He and his family attracted a large customer base that was a major factor in the market's revival.

Jack McDavid bought the old Glass House Restaurant in the market and turned it into the Down Home Diner. Here Jack takes a break in front of the ersatz "Signing of the Declaration of Independence" mural that was painted in 1947 and hung in the restrooms on the train floor when the headhouse was modernized. After the train shed closed, many benches, signs, fixtures, baggage carts, and memorabilia were recycled for use in the market.   *Courtesy of Burk Uzzle.*

Delilah Winder started in Reading Terminal Market in the mid-1980s and has gone on to become one of the most successful restaurateurs in the city, with additional locations on lower Market Street and at the airport. Delilah serves southern-style cuisine. *Courtesy of Anne Day.*

John Yi's fish stand has one of the largest selections of fish and seafood in the city. It is owned and operated by John Yi and Suzie Kim, both of whom emigrated from Korea. Suzie is a concert pianist but devotes most of her time today to fish scales, not musical ones.   *Courtesy of Anne Day.*

Rick Olivieri's family invented the cheesesteak, and today Rick oversees the business in the market that was started by his father, Herbert Olivieri.   *Courtesy of Anne Day.*

Julia Child was one of many famous chefs who visited the market in the 1980s. She stopped by Ochs's stall to get some tips about butterflying a lamb.   *Courtesy of WHYY.*

Alice Waters, local-food advocate and restaurateur extraordinaire, sets up a market stall with organic produce from California on one of the old baggage carts from the train shed. She appeared at the market in 1988.

The neon arrow pointing down Twelfth Street was an important symbol for market aficionados wandering down Market Street from the west. It was located on the corner alcove, just above the Reading Company president's office. The neon sign is now gone and the corner has sprouted a giant neon guitar for the franchise restaurant that occupies the ground-floor corner of the headhouse.

Trompe l'oeil murals and vignettes by artist Liddy Lindsay were used throughout the market to hide walk-in boxes and decorate blank walls. This mural depicts Spataro's old lunch counter, and the eggs in front are real.   *Courtesy of Burk Uzzle.*

An editorial cartoon from April 1989 by Signe Wilkinson of the *Philadelphia Daily News* spoofed what could happen to Reading Terminal Market once the Convention Center was built. During the late 1980s there was much debate about the effect that thousands of tourists would have on the day-to-day life of the market.   *Courtesy of Signe Wilkinson,* Philadelphia Daily News.

The two-square-block footprint for the Pennsylvania Convention Center was leveled one building at a time.

The wrecking ball has cleared the landscape at Twelfth and Arch Streets many times over the last one hundred and fifty years. Here, in 1989, the razers are at work tearing down the old train viaduct and buildings in the blocks to the north of Reading Terminal Market to make way for the Convention Center.

The Pennsylvania Convention Center's ambitious plans threatened the revived market and a grassroots campaign was launched to gather public support to "save" it. This button was designed by *Philadelphia Inquirer* cartoonist Tony Auth and was sold to raise funds for the merchants' effort to get the support of City Council to keep the market open and vital during the construction of the half-billion-dollar Convention Center project.

The magnificent shed saw its last train in 1984, and the emptied space had to be fully cleaned of residue before the sale of the property to the Convention Center could be made final. The clean-up entailed removal of the tracks and track beds and caused major leaks into the market.

The train shed as it looked in the late 1980s during the clean-up phase, just before it was sold to the Convention Center.   *Courtesy of Eli Albalancey.*

On February 22, 1992, Reading Terminal Market was a century young. PECO Energy celebrated the occasion by putting the market's name in lights for all to see.
Courtesy of PECO Energy.

Noelle Margerum, William Margerum's great-great-granddaughter, operated a specialty grocery stall for many years. Her old-fashioned bins and scoops were part of the show that brought customers back generation after generation. The health department forced her to stop using the bins in the 1990s, and they were replaced with plastic, laminated ones. *Courtesy of Burk Uzzle.*

After 109 years, the Margerum family left Reading Terminal Market. This photo was taken the last day their stall was open, July 1, 2001, and shows Carole Margerum preparing some herbs for a customer.

Many elderly customers who live in Philadelphia were raised on farms and appreciate the variety of locally raised products available at the market.
Courtesy of Burk Uzzle.

Outdoor seating is a new feature in front of the restaurant on the ground floor of the parking garage at Twelfth and Filbert Streets. The new buildings on this block have a greater setback than the previous buildings, giving Twelfth Street a more open and inviting feel.

Two views, taken twenty years apart, looking down Twelfth Street. The photo on the top was taken in 1980; the one on the bottom, in 2000. The investment of hundreds of millions of dollars in two decades has dramatically changed the area, and the market struggles to keep its local customer base as thousands of conventioneers and tourists now fill the aisles at lunchtime.

NOTES

1. From *The Casket*, June 1828, quoted in Agnes Addison Gilchrist, "Market Houses in High Street," *Trans. American Philosophical Society* 43, pt. 1 (1953): 304-312.

2. *Writings of Benjamin Franklin*, ed. A. H. Smyth (New York: Macmillan, 1906), 11: 511.

3. Charles Poulson, *Scrapbook* 9 (1857): 37.

4. Ibid., 1 (10 April 1859): 67.

5. "Two Historic 12th St. Institutions Must Go," *Philadelphia Times*, 14 February 1892.

6. Archibald Angus McLeod to Twelfth Street Market Company, 3 August 1891, 12th Street Market Company Minutes, Hagley Museum and Library.

7. Helen Tangires, "The Life and Death of Center Market," *Washington History. Magazine* 7, no. 1 (1995): 59

8. "A Mammoth Arch," *Philadelphia Record*, September 1891.

9. Food show program, Reading Terminal Market Merchants Association, February 1934, 7.

10. Ibid.

11. Madelin Blitzstein, "Terminal Firms Supply Delicacies to Customers in 38 States," *Philadelphia Evening Bulletin*, 24 July 1932.

12. Beeber Gross, Reading Company Archives, Hagley Museum and Library, Greenville, Del.

13. "Lady Butcher's Carols Enthrall Market Patrons," *Philadelphia Evening Bulletin*, 22 December 1960.

14. John Keats, "Market: The Golden Age Has Never Really Passed," *Sunday Bulletin Magazine*, 20 January 1963.

15. Cartoon flyer published by Pennsylvania Railroad, 1894.

16. Rem Rieder, "Reading Terminal Market Future Is Cloudy," *Philadelphia Evening Bulletin*, 6 April 1975.

17. David Esh, quoting his father Samuel, in an interview with the author.

18. *Writings of Benjamin Franklin*, 11: 511.

19. William R. Dimeling, in an interview with the author.

SELECTED BIBLIOGRAPHY

Books

Barshinger, Jay R. *Provisions for Trade: The Market House in Southeastern Pennsylvania.* Ph.D. diss., Pennsylvania State University, 1995.

De Voe, Thomas. *The Market Assistant.* New York: Hurd and Houghton, 1867.

Enos, D. G. *Official Market Directory and Family Cookbook.* Philadelphia: Dunlap Printing Company, n.d.

Holton, James L. *The Reading Railroad: History of a Coal Age Empire.* 2 vols. Laury's Station, PA: Garrigues House, 1989–92.

Jackson, Joseph. *Market Street.* Philadelphia: Patterson and White, 1918.

Lippincott, Horace Mather. *Early Philadelphia, Its People, Life and Progress.* Philadelphia: J. B. Lippincott, 1917.

Moore, Edwin Coutant. *The House of Excellence.* Philadelphia: William B. Margerum, 1931.

Reading Company. *This Is the Reading.* Philadelphia: Reading Company, 1958.

Scharf, J. Thomas, and Thompson Westcott. *History of Philadelphia 1609–1884.* Philadelphia: L. H. Everts & Co., 1884.

Smyth, A. H., ed. 1906. *Writings of Benjamin Franklin.* New York: Macmillan.

Strahan, Edward. *A Century After: Picturesque Glimpses of Philadelphia and Pennsylvania.* Philadelphia: Allen, Lane & Scott and J. W. Lauderbach, 1875.

Tangires, Helen. *Public Markets and Civic Culture in Nineteenth-Century America.* Baltimore: Johns Hopkins University Press, 2003.

Westcott, Thompson. *Guide Book to Philadelphia.* Philadelphia: Porter and Coates, 1876.

Weygandt, Cornelius. *Philadelphia Folks.* New York: D. Appleton–Century, 1938.

Periodicals

Blitzstein, Madelin. "Terminal Firms Supply Delicacies to Customers in 38 States." *Philadelphia Evening Bulletin,* 24 July 1932.

Gilchrist, Agnes Addison. "Market Houses in High Street." *Trans. American Philosophical Society* 43, pt. 1 (1953): 304–312.

Keats, John. "Market: The Golden Age Has Never Really Passed." *Sunday Bulletin Magazine,* 20 January 1963.

National Railway Historical Society. "Reading Terminal, Philadelphia, 1893–1968." *The Bulletin* 33, no. 6 (1968).

Philadelphia Evening Bulletin. "Lady Butcher's Carols Enthrall Market Patrons." 22 December 1960.

Philadelphia Record. 1 September 1891–1 December 1893.

Philadelphia Record. "A Mammoth Arch." September 1891.

Philadelphia Times. "Two Historic 12th St. Institutions Must Go." 14 February 1892.

Poulson, Charles. *Scrapbook.* Library Company of Philadelphia.

Reading Company Technical and Historical Society. *The Bee Line* 7, no. 1 (1985).

Rieder, Rem. "Reading Terminal Market Future Is Cloudy." *Philadelphia Evening Bulletin.* 6 April 1975.

Sunday Bulletin Magazine. "Market: The Golden Age Has Never Really Passed." 20 January 1960.

Tangires, Helen. "The Life and Death of Center Market." *Washington History Magazine* 7, no. 1 (1995): 46–67.

Archives and Collections

Campbell Collection. Historical files. Historical Society of Pennsylvania. Philadelphia.

Historical files. Atwater Kent Museum. Philadelphia.

Historical files. Library Company of Philadelphia.

Historical files. Temple University Urban Archives. Philadelphia.

Perkins Collection. Historical files. Historical Society of Pennsylvania. Philadelphia.

Philadelphia *Bulletin* Archives. Temple University Urban Archives. Philadelphia.

Reading Company Archives. Athenaeum of Philadelphia.

Reading Company Archives. Hagley Museum and Library. Greenville, Del.

Of Related Interest

The Reading Terminal Market Cookbook
Ann Hazan and Irina Smith

The Reading Terminal Market Cookbook, the perfect companion to the history of the market, will allow you to bring its delicious specialties to your own table. All of the merchants share treasured recipes that can be created easily with ingredients readily available at their stalls. This cookbook also celebrates the dedication of the merchants, the loyalty of customers, and the diversity of the cultures and neighborhoods that this historic market serves.

The Original Philadelphia Neighborhood Cookbook
Irina Smith and Ann Hazan

Philadelphia, a city of neighborhoods, now has a cookbook that represents the rich culinary tastes and practices of its residents. The authors have collected a wealth of easy-to-prepare, kitchen-tested dishes for all occasions and times of day. Each recipe includes ethnic origins and background commentary as well as serving suggestions and variations.

The *Philadelphia Inquirer*'s Guide to Historic Philadelphia
Edward Colimore   2nd Edition

Here is an indispensable guide for visitors to Philadelphia, for residents who want to know more about their city's past, and for anyone who has an interest in the history of one of our country's oldest and greatest cities. Aided by maps and detailed itineraries, the history buff can follow twelve walks through neighborhoods where the buildings, streets, gardens, and parks—dating from the colonial period to the Victorian era—still stand as proud testaments to the city's storied past.

CAMINO BOOKS, INC.
P. O. Box 59026
Philadelphia, PA 19102

Please send me:

_____ copy(ies) of *The Reading Terminal Market: An Illustrated History,* $19.95

_____ copy(ies) of *The Reading Terminal Market Cookbook,* $16.95

_____ copy(ies) of *The Original Philadelphia Neighborhood Cookbook,* $16.95

_____ copy(ies) of *The* Philadelphia Inquirer*'s Guide to Historic Philadelphia,* $14.95

Name _____

Address _____

City/State/Zip _____

All orders must be prepaid. Your satisfaction is guaranteed. You can return the books for a full refund. Please add $5.95 for postage and handling for the first book and $1.00 for each additional.

78-3